ROCK CLIMBING IN IRELAND

Disclaimer

The writer and publisher of this book accepts no responsibility for the way in which readers use the information contained therein. The descriptions and recommendations are for guidance only and must be subject to discriminating judgement by the reader. Advice and training should be sought before utilising any equipment or techniques mentioned within the text or shown in any of the photographic images. Climbing is an activity with a danger of personal injury or death. Participants should be aware of, and accept, these risks and be responsible for their own actions and involvement. The inclusion of a climbing area in this guidebook does not mean you have a right of access or the right to climb upon it.

Published by Three Rock Books
www.threerockbooks.com
info@threerockbooks.com

Printed in Poland
LF Book Services

ISBN 978-0-9567874-2-2

All photos by author unless credited.
Front cover: John McCune on the first ascent of The Second Coming E7 (5c,6b), Owey Island, Donegal (see page 187). Photo by Craig Hiller.
Back cover: Marek Belopotocky on Thunderhips E1 5b, Fair Head, Antrim (see page 233). Photo by Juraj Navratil.

ROCK CLIMBING IN IRELAND

David Flanagan

Three **Rock** **Books**

This guidebook is dedicated to the memory of Colm Ennis and Peter Britton who died a few months before this book was published in an accident descending from the Dent du Géant in the French Alps.

CONTENTS

INTRODUCTION

Ireland is blessed with a wealth of amazing traditional climbing. Many of the best crags are in some of the wildest, most beautiful places in the country where solitude is almost guaranteed and queuing for a route, no matter how classic, is unheard of.

The rich diversity of climbing and the wide range of rock types give each area a unique character and there are quality routes throughout the grades with classics from Diff to E9. It's no exaggeration to say that Ireland has something for every climber whatever their ability and taste.

Ireland's best-known climbing areas - Ailladie and Fair Head - are attracting visitors from abroad in increasing numbers and deservedly so as they both offer steep, physical climbing of the highest quality. However, there are many other excellent crags that aren't as well-known but are just as worthy of a visit, such as the Gap of Dunloe in Kerry, Luggala in Wicklow and Gola Island in Donegal.

Whether you are visiting Ireland on a climbing holiday or a native looking to venture beyond your local crags I hope that you will find this book both inspiring and informative.

THIS SPREAD Marek Belopotocky on Thunderhips E1 5b, Fair Head, Antrim (see page 233). Photo by Juraj Navratil.
PREVIOUS SPREAD Sean Villanueva O'Driscoll on The Cabbage E2 6a, Muckros Head, Donegal (see page 155). Photo by Ben Ditto.

North West Donegal
• Cruit Island
• Owey Island
• Gola Island

South West Donegal
• Muckros Head
• Sail Rock
• Malin Beg
• Cnoc na Mara

Inishowen

Fair Head

DERRY

Lough Barra

Lough Belshade

BELFAST

Mournes
• Pigeon Rock
• Hen Mountain
• Binnian North Tor
• Buzzard's Roost
• Spellack
• Bearnagh Slabs
• Slieve Beg
• Annalong Buttress
• Lower Cove
• Slieve Lamagan

Ben Corr

GALWAY

DUBLIN
Dalkey Quarry

Ailladie

Luggala

Glendalough
Glenmalure

LIMERICK   KILKENNY

WATERFORD

Dún
Séanna
Head

Coumshingaun

Gap of Dunloe
Carrauntoohil

CORK   50km

10

HOW TO USE THIS BOOK

This book documents the best of Irish climbing and I'm confident that there is more than enough top-quality routes in this book to keep the vast majority of climbers occupied for a long time.

Areas are listed in clockwise order, starting in Dublin and routes are described from left to right facing the crag. North is the top of the page in all the maps.

Each crag has an introduction which outlines the approach and descent, advises on conditions and any particular equipment requirements. The best routes are described in detail and in certain cases other routes are mentioned in passing, these mightn't be of the very highest quality but are still worth climbing. If you are spending an extended period in an area it may be worth purchasing the definitive guide, see details on page 285.

If you are planning to travel around the country a GPS or road map is vital as signposting can often be nonexistent and many crags are accessed via small, obscure roads. Probably the best approach is to download the crag locations from www.rockClimbingInIreland.com onto your GPS or smartphone and use that to navigate.

On page 22 there is a table that gives an overview of all the crags which should be helpful when trip planning.

Conditions

North facing crags are cold and rarely get any sun (even in the summer), hence they can be very slow to dry and are often quite vegetated. South facing crags get the sun all day, but they are exposed to the southwesterly wind. East facing cliffs only get sun early in the day while a west facing cliff will get the afternoon and evening sun.

SAFETY

Climbing on large crags in the mountains and on sea cliffs can be extremely committing and if you have any doubts about what you are doing you should seek professional instruction or hire a guide.

Before setting out:

- Get a detailed weather forecast. Check the tides if relevant.
- Ensure that you and your equipment are up to the task.
- Carry enough emergency equipment to keep you comfortable should you get hurt and need to stop moving.
- Leave word with someone responsible.
- Carry a fully charged mobile phone.

Mountain Routes

Many of the climbs in this book are in remote, mountainous areas where there is no phone coverage and the weather can change very quickly. You should be equipped for bad weather and prepared to navigate in bad conditions. Wear appropriate footwear, and carry waterproofs, emergency rations, head torch, map and compass.

Sea Cliffs

Climbing near the sea, especially when the routes must be accessed by abseil requires particular skills and poses some unique risks. The tide and the state of the sea are very important so

always consult tide tables and check the weather forecast before you climb. While climbing keep an eye on the sea conditions and watch out for rouge waves which can sweep across rock platforms without warning. When an abseil is required to reach the start of the climb it's best practise to leave the abseil rope in place as an escape route.

Mountain Rescue

In an emergency, call 999 or 112 and ask the emergency operator for "Mountain Rescue". You will then be put through to a Gardaí or PSNI station where the situation will be assessed and, if necessary, a mountain rescue team called out.

Fixed Equipment

Some older routes may sport a peg or two. Usually these are in a bad state and can't be relied upon. You may very rarely encounter a bolt but these are usually more modern and more reliable. Some crags are equipped with in-situ anchors for abseiling, usually chains or stakes but sometimes bolts. These are of varying quality and age and it's up to each climber to satisfy themselves that they are trustworthy before using them. If in doubt don't trust them.

EQUIPMENT

A standard traditional rack will suffice for most routes. If a route has any very specific or unusual protection requirements they will be mentioned in the description. While not essential double ropes are very useful, they also make abseil descents or retreats more efficient. For most pitches 50m ropes are sufficient.

Whether you choose to wear a helmet

or not is personal choice but on some of the looser routes it would be extremely unwise not to do so.

ACCESS AND CONSERVATION

Currently there is no formal right to public access of private land in Ireland. However the majority of rural landowners have traditionally granted access to mountain and crag areas. Be considerate and polite in any dealings with landowners. Park carefully - make sure not to block access and leave gates as you find them. Avoid taking dogs to any area where sheep or cattle may be grazing.

The following guidelines are based on Mountaineering Ireland's *Good Practice Guide*:

- Cliffs are a final refuge for some plants, birds and animals that have become rare, or even extinct elsewhere.
- Avoid disturbing nesting birds and adhere to any climbing restrictions during the nesting season.
- The removal of vegetation including mosses and lichens (gardening) should be avoided wherever possible.
- Damage can be caused by repeated top-roping of routes or by using a wire brush for cleaning.
- Avoid any form of chipping or defacement of the rock.
- Abseiling down routes can be harmful to the rock, damage vegetation and inhibit other climbers.
- Where abseiling from trees is necessary, use a rope protector.

Mountaineering Ireland

INFORMATION FOR VISITORS

Ireland is an ideal destination for a climbing holiday. It has a wide range of rock types and a good variety of climbing styles and areas, but the county is still small enough that it's possible to drive the length of it in a day.

Ireland has become popular as an adventure sports destination. In recent years its surf has been recognised as world class and there is a huge amount of excellent hiking and mountain biking. So don't despair if it does rain, there is plenty to keep you occupied.

There is also plenty of more sedate tourist attractions, check out www.discoverireland.ie for more information.

When To Visit?

While the Irish climate isn't particularly extreme (heavy snowfall or extended dry spells are rare) it is unpredictable. We have seasons but the weather doesn't pay a massive amount of attention to them. Of course the winter is generally colder than the summer but that's about all you can say with any certainty.

There isn't a climbing season as such and in theory it's possible to climb all year around, particular at the more sheltered crags, but it's often too cold or damp to climb on the mountain crags outside of summer. Seepage can also be an issue, some of the bigger more vegetated crags need a few days of dry weather to come into condition.

The warmer, longer summer days (in late June the sun doesn't set until half ten) are the most popular time to climb in Ireland. Bear in mind that midges (tiny flying insects that feast on humans) can be a problem on still, humid days between May and September. They are abundant in the mountains but less common in coastal areas. Seek out exposed areas as once there is a breeze there is no problem. It's worth carrying a head-net just in case.

A climbing trip to any temperate region contains an element of risk but a lot of that risk can be mitigated by being flexible and making good, informed choices about where to climb. Ireland is a small country, so move around to take advantage of better weather. Don't take good weather for granted and don't have too much faith in the forecast.

Take advantage of dry spells by climbing in the mountains. If the weather is more changeable then the coastal crags are the best option. They tend to get better weather than areas only a few miles inland but wind and swell are extra factors that need to be considered.

Getting To Ireland

Ireland's main airport is in Dublin, but it's also possible to fly into one of the smaller airports in the north or west (Belfast, Shannon and Kerry).

The ferry is a good option for visitors from the UK but it can be expensive especially during the summer. There are five major ferry ports along the east coast - Larne, Belfast, Dublin, Dun Laoghaire and Rosslare.

Transport

Visiting most of the climbing areas in this guide requires a car, however car hire is relatively cheap. When parking in remote areas make sure that you don't leave any valuables in the car, break-ins can be a problem particularly in the Wicklow Mountains.

It's possible to travel between cities by train (see www.irishrail.ie) and between towns by bus (see www.buseireann.ie) but as most of the climbing is in remote rural areas the last leg of the journey can be a challenge.

Partners

The climbing scene is Ireland is small and quite localised. If you are without a climbing partner don't rely on showing up at the crag and finding one. You are much better off posting on the forum at www.climbing.ie.

Provisions

Every city in Ireland has an outdoor shop where you can get chalk and other climbing equipment. See the list of advertisers on page 287

Accommodation

Ireland is well equipped with hostels, bed and breakfasts, campsites and hotels. If staying in one area for more than a few days it can be quite economical to rent a house.

Wild Camping

Ireland has great potential for wild camping. Ideally permission should be sought from the landowner before

camping, however this often isn't practical. The best approach is to keep a low profile by putting the tent up late and taking it down early.

Water from small lakes and streams up high is usually drinkable though you never can tell if there is a dead sheep rotting a few hundred metres upstream!

Maps

The entire island of Ireland is covered at a scale of 1:50,000 by the Discovery/ Discoverer series published in the Republic by OSI and in the North by Land & Property Services. It would be wise to carry the relevant map if you are climbing at any of the more remote mountain crags.

Climbing Walls

Only in recent years have Irish climbing walls started to catch up with international standards. The following is a list of dedicated climbing centres:

- Awesome Walls, Dublin (see advertisement on page 20).
- Gravity Climbing Centre, Dublin (see advertisement on page 12).
- Ozone, Belfast.
- Boulder Belfast.
- Awesome Walls, Cork (see advertisement on page 20).
- Hot Rock, Tollymore, Down.
- Play at Height, Dingle, Kerry.

There are many other smaller climbing walls scattered across the country, for a link to a list of walls see page 285.

FACING PAGE David Lyons Ewing on Warhorse E4 6a, Spellack, Mournes, Down (see page 259). Photo by Thomas Prebble.

Sport Climbing

Until recently a strict ethic of leader
placed protection prevailed, as a result
the development of sport climbing in
Ireland has been slow and very low-key.

Bouldering

The Irish climate and geology is quite
suited to bouldering and it has become
very popular in recent years. Those bitter
winter days when it's too cold for 'real
climbing' are ideal for bouldering. Some
of the best bouldering areas include:

- Glendalough, Wicklow. Probably
  the best area in Ireland. With over
  150 problems packed into the valley
  there is an unrivalled density of
  boulder problems. There are also
  plenty of other smaller, high quality
  areas nearby.

- The Gap of Dunloe, Kerry. Between
  the Gap and the nearby Black Valley
  there are about 100 problems on
  fantastic sandstone.
- Doolin, Clare. The limestone walls
  contain over 80 problems and are
  close to the village of Doolin which is
  a handy base for Ailladie.
- Donegal has a large number of very
  pleasant smaller areas but no single
  outstanding destination.
- Fair Head, Antrim. The extensive
  boulder fields below the crag
  contains nearly 500 problems. The
  rock is steep and the holds are small
  making the Head one of the best
  areas in Ireland for hard bouldering

For more information check out
Bouldering in Ireland by David Flanagan.

FACING PAGE Tim Chapman bouldering in
Glendalough, Wicklow.

19

Ireland's biggest and best indoor climbing centers in Dublin and Cork

AWESOME WALLS
CLIMBING CENTRES

coaching
beginner classes
equipment shop
café / group rates
info@awesomewalls.ie
www.awesomewalls.ie

Grades

In Ireland the British scale for traditional protected climbs is used. This system consists of two grades, an adjective and a technical one.

The adjectival grade describes the overall difficulty of the climb taking into account factors such as exposure, protection, rock quality and how sustained the climbing is. The range, in order of difficulty is - Difficult, Very Difficult, Severe, Hard Severe, Very Severe, Hard Very Severe, Extremely severe (which is further divided into E1,E2 etc. up to E11)

The technical grade describes the difficulty of the hardest move (3c, 4a, 4b, 4c, 5a, 5b, 5c, 6a, 6b, 6c, 7a).

By analysing the relationship between the two grades it's possible to learn more about the nature of the climbing. For example VS 4c is a typical grade, hence VS 4b implies either poor protection or sustained climbing, while VS 5a would usually indicate a difficult but well-protected crux.

While grades offer only a rough indication of difficulty, most of the routes in this guide are long established and reasonably popular so the grades should be relatively accurate.

The table on the right compares the various international grading systems, it should give visitors who are unfamiliar with this grading system some idea of what to expect. However any comparison between well bolted sport routes and sparsely protected traditional climbs should taken with a pinch of salt.

UK	US	French
D	5.2	2
VD	5.3/5.4	2+,3
S	5.5/5.6	3+
HS	5.6/5.7	4
VS	5.8	4+
HVS	5.9/5.10a	5/5+
E1	5.10b	6a
E2	5.10c/d	6a+/6b
E3	5.11a	6b+
E4	5.11b/c	6c/6c+
E5	5.11d-5.12b	7a-7b
E6	5.12c-5.13a	7b+-7c+
E7	5.13b-5.13c	7c/7c+
E8	5.13d/5.14a	8b/8b+
E9	5.14b/5.14c	8c/8c+

CRAG TABLE

CRAG	ROUTES	D-S	HS-HVS	E1-E3	E4+
Dalkey Quarry	26	4	12	8	2
Luggala	16	1	5	9	1
Glendalough	24	1	16	6	1
Glenmalure	1	0	1	0	0
Coumshingaun	17	0	6	8	3
Carrauntoohil	1	1	0	0	0
Gap of Dunloe	44	1	23	18	2
Dún Séanna Head	16	1	10	3	2
Ailladie	43	0	7	19	17
Ben Corr	1	1	0	0	0
Muckros Head	18	1	6	7	4
Sail Rock	2	0	1	1	0
Malin Beg	7	1	6	0	0
Cnoc na Mara	1	0	1	0	0
Lough Belshade	6	0	4	2	0
Lough Barra	6	1	2	3	0
Cruit Island	22	10	6	6	0
Owey Island	5	0	1	1	3
Gola Island	26	4	9	9	4
Fair Head	41	0	8	26	7
Mournes - Pigeon Rock	9	1	4	4	0
Mournes - Hen Mountain	17	3	5	9	0
Mournes - Binnian North Tor	8	1	4	2	1
Mournes - Buzzard's Roost	4	1	0	0	3
Mournes - Spellack	5	1	1	1	2
Mournes - Bearnagh Slabs	4	2	1	1	0
Mournes - Slieve Beg	9	1	4	4	0
Mournes - Annalong Buttress	13	7	6	0	0
Mournes - Lower Cove	14	2	4	6	2
Mournes - Slieve Lamagan	2	1	1	0	0

WALK-IN (minutes)	ROCK	STYLE	SETTING	ORIENTATION	PAGE
5	Granite	Single	Quarry	N,E,W	25
45	Granite	Both	Mountain	S,E	40
50	Granite	Both	Mountain	S	57
60	Granite	Multi	Mountain	SW	75
45	Conglomerate	Both	Mountain	N	79
120	Sandstone	Multi	Mountain	N,E	91
1-30	Sandstone	Both	Valley	E,W	97
15	Sandstone	Single	Sea Cliff, non-tidal	S	117
5	Limestone	Single	Sea Cliff, partially tidal	W	127
75	Quartzite	Multi	Mountain	N	149
2	Sandstone	Single	Sea Cliff, partially tidal	S	155
20	Quartzite	Multi	Sea Cliff, non-tidal	S	163
5	Quartzite	Single	Sea Cliff, partially tidal	W	165
180	Choss	Multi	Sea Stack, non-tidal	E	169
120	Granite	Multi	Mountain	E	174
20	Granite	Both	Mountain	S,E	181
1	Granite	Single	Sea Cliff, partially tidal	S	184
45	Granite	Multi	Sea Cliff, non-tidal	N,W	187
45	Granite	Single	Sea Cliff, partially tidal	S,W	191
20-45	Dolerite	Both	Lowland	N,E,W	204
10	Granite	Both	Valley	E	239
20	Granite	Single	Mountain	E,W	244
90	Granite	Single	Mountain	S,W	249
60	Granite	Multi	Mountain	E	253
30	Granite	Single	Mountain	E	257
60	Granite	Multi	Mountain	NW	260
90	Granite	Both	Mountain	S	262
75	Granite	Single	Mountain	W	274
60	Granite	Both	Mountain	S	269
60	Granite	Multi	Mountain	S	255

County Dublin

DALKEY QUARRY

APPROACH **5 minutes**
ROCK **Granite**
D-S **4** - HS-HVS **12** - E1-E3 **8** - E4+ **2**

Dalkey Quarry is one the most popular climbing areas in Ireland and while it doesn't represent the very best of Irish climbing, as urban quarries go it's pretty good. It's very convenient for Dublin-based climbers on summer evenings and for visitors who are entering or leaving the country via Dublin.

The vast majority of routes in the Quarry are single-pitch. The easier climbs tend to feature distinct cruxes between easier ground while the harder routes are usually steeper and more sustained. The rock quality is variable, ranging from immaculate white granite to rotten orange choss, but for the most part it's good.

The boreholes left by the quarrymen take a bomber size #3 tricam.

CONDITIONS

With walls facing north, west and east it's always possible to find shade or sun as required. The lower quarries, particularly the more sheltered West Valley, are the best option on cold, windy days. Some lines seep during the winter but it's possible to climb year-round.

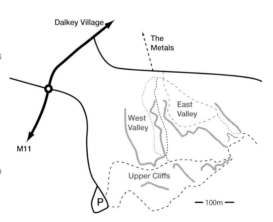

DIRECTIONS

The DART (train) runs regularly from the city centre to Dalkey Village leaving a 10 minute walk to the Quarry. Leave the station and follow the road uphill, crossing over the tracks. Take the first turn right. At the T-junction at the top of the steep road turn right. At the next T-junction turn left. After 40m there is a narrow lane on the left, known as The Metals, which leads to the lower entrance of the Quarry.

Travelling by car from the M50 take exit 16 and, following signs for Dún Laoghaire, cross over the N11. After 500m turn right (signposted 'Killiney'), go straight on for 800m and turn left (signposted 'Killiney'). Take the first exit off the roundabout, pass Killiney Castle Hotel, at the next roundabout take the last exit and drive up the steep road to the carpark. A tarmac path leads from the carpark into the Quarry.

FACING PAGE Brian Hall on The Ghost E2 5b (see page 32). Photo by Richard Creagh.

UPPER CLIFFS

The Upper Cliffs are home to some of the longest routes in the Quarry. The rock is high quality particularly on Central Buttress and White Wall. As the cliffs face north they tend to get a lot of shade so they can be slow to dry after a wet spell.

1 **Great Central Route** E3 6a   27m

Well protected climbing. Climb the rib easily to a stance and peg. Pass the peg and make a tenuous move left around the arete to the recess. Bridge up the recess to better finishing holds. **Maricon** E3 5c is similar in style, if a little easier.
R. Richardson, J. Lynam 1975
After loss of a block - D. O'Sullivan 20/08/1990

Central Buttress is the steep outcrop to the right. The left arete is taken by **Slapstick** E7 6b one of the hardest routes in the Quarry.

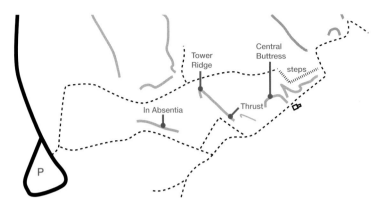

2 **Central Buttress** E1 (5b,4b) — 37m

The line of least resistance up the middle of the wall. Approach the start from the left hand side.

P1 30m From the left end of the ledge make steep technical moves (crux) up the rib to another ledge. Step up and traverse left to a large ledge below a hanging block in a corner. Climb the corner steeply to another ledge. Traverse left around the corner and make a long step to the belay ledge.

P2 7m Move left and up into a small overhanging V-corner. Finish up the slab.
F. Maguire, J. Morrison, P. Kenny 1951

Hari Kari Groove E3 5c breaks out right from Central Buttress at the ledge below the hanging block and follows a series of grooves before a spectacular finish through the roofs.

3 **Port Cullis** E4 6a — 35m

A well protected technical route. Climb the groove to the square roof and traverse left past a peg to a pocket and crack. A hard move leads to a rest and another peg at the foot of a white slab. Climb the slab, moving right at the top into a hanging groove. Finish up the groove and belay at the tree.
H. Hebblethwaite, D. O'Sullivan August 1985

4 **Astrodog** E2 5c — 30m

Slightly chossy rock but with enjoyable, pumpy climbing. Start just right of the quartz vein. Follow good holds diagonally right to a crack in the corner. Climb the crack to hard moves where it joins the quartz vein at a small quartz nose. Climb the chimney above passing a peg until it's possible to step left onto a large ledge. Finish over the bulge in a fine situation.
T. Burke, D. O'Sullivan August 1983

TOWER RIDGE

5 **Thrust** HVS 5a 24m

A brilliant route that is best done in one long, well-protected pitch. Start at the foot of the left-facing corner. Climb the corner passing an awkward section near the top. Move up and right on flakes to the base of a slab split by a thin crack (optional belay). Climb the thin crack (crux) to a ledge. Follow the good holds up and left to belay at the tree.
G. Jones, P. Duggan 30/12/1968
Direct finish - T. Ryan, S. Windrim 31/12/1976

6 **Crime In The City** E4 6a 15m

Absorbing climbing and well protected where it matters. Climb to the overlap and move left to a good flat hold (peg). Continue with difficulty to a narrow ledge and make thin moves past two pegs to better holds. Traverse right across the top of a short corner to a ledge. Finish up the diagonal crack.
C. O'Cofaigh, H. Hebblethwaite, B. Callan 20/06/1989

7 **Giant's Staircase** S (3c,3a)   26m

The stepped wall under the large overhang. Stays reasonably dry in the rain.
P1   20m Start at the yew tree. Climb the series of ledges, initially keeping to the right, near the overhang, the last step is the hardest. Belay just before the corner.
P2   6m Carefully climb the loose corner to join and finish up Tower Ridge.
P1 IMC. Early 1940s.
P2 A. Kopczynski, J. Morrison 1952

8 **Graham Crackers** HVS 5a   22m

Superb bold climbing. Start directly below the thin crack of Tower Ridge Direct. Climb the wall to an awkward mantel. Move left over ledges to a borehole right of the nose. A hard move gains a standing position on top of the nose (very small nuts). Step right and boldly climb the wall to the horizontal break. Move left and up a wall to a ledge. Finish up Tower Ridge. Two tricams are useful for the boreholes.
R. Richardson, P. McMenamin, C. Richardson May 1975

The Prisoner E5 6a breaks out left from Graham Crackers.

9 **Cell Block H** E1 5b   30m

Start as for Graham Crackers. Climb the wall and then move up over ledges to the base of a groove. Step left and climb a second very shallow groove (easier than it looks) to the horizontal crack. Follow this for 10m to a fingery finish up the thin crack.
D. O'Sullivan, J. Lyons 14/08/1990

10 **Tower Ridge Direct** E2 5c   18m

Well protected. Start as for Graham Crackers but move up and right over ledges to the base of the thin crack. Climb the crack and belay as for P1 of Tower Ridge.
Unknown 1952
FFA W. Lee 1980

11 **Tower Ridge** D   40m

Enjoyable easy climbing up the ridge.
P1   21m Start on the right side of the ridge and climb the groove on orange rock. Move left once the angle eases and shuffle to the end of the ledge. Mantle onto the slab and belay where the crack splits the short wall above.
P2   19m Climb the crack then hand traverse across the wonderfully exposed ridge. Finish by scrambling over the short walls and corners to belay at the stone wall.
IMC Early 1940s

⑫

⑬ Hyperior

WHITE WALL

White Wall is the first outcrop on the right when you enter the quarry from the main carpark. The rock is immaculate white granite and the climbing is intense, balancy and exposed.

12 **Helios** VS 4c   34m

Testing. Start just left of the vertical, black streaked wall at the left end of the cliff. Move up over ledges passing a steep step (bisected by a vertical borehole) on the left (easier) or right. Climb the groove above and step right onto the narrow ledge (tricam in the borehole). Move up the groove to a peg and step left onto an exposed stance on the notch in the left arete. Either move directly up or step right across the void. Pass the triangular nose on its left and move right onto the easy slab. Belay at the tree.
P. Kenny, A. Kopczynski 1951

13 **In Absentia** HVS 5a   20m

Good climbing with a worrying crux. Start 6m right of Helios at the large ash tree. Follow the groove to a grassy ledge. Continue up to a sloping ledge and traverse left across the ledge to a triangular nose. Make very precarious moves around the nose. Climb onto the top of the nose and finish boldly up the wall above. Belay at the tree.
A. Kopczynski, R. Ohrtmann 1952

To the right of In Absentia is **Hyperion** VS 4c which climbs a line just left of the overhanging wall. The climbing is uneventful until the last few moves stepping out onto the slab.

EAST VALLEY

The east side of the East Valley is a sun trap and very sheltered. Descent from the following two routes by scrambling down the ramp to the left.

14 **Street Fighter** VS 4c   12m

Steep climbing with good protection. Climb the groove on jugs to a ledge. Step left onto a narrow, sloping ramp, and follow the thin crack to the top.
K. Higgs, S. Young 29/05/1976

Erewhon E2 5b climbs the wall left of Street Fighter linking the three boreholes.

15 **The Shield** E2 5c   15m

A classic battle, much fallen off. Follow Street Fighter to the ledge and jam up the crack on the right.
S. Young 1973
FFA S. Windrim 22/04/1978

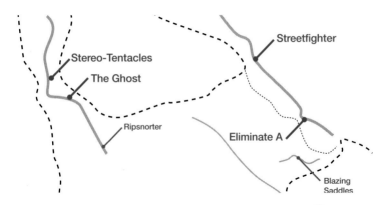

The slab at the far right end of the wall is known as the Eliminates. It's covered in holds and it's possible to climb nearly anywhere on it at around VD but one route stands out.

16 **Eliminate A** VD   15m

Very enjoyable climbing up the left arete of the slab. Start at the bottom left corner of the slab. Climb the left edge of the slab (bold but easy) to a stance below the vertical wall. Follow the thin crack on good jugs to the top.
IMC Early 1940s

Directly opposite the Eliminates is a small steep buttress split by three cracks. The left crack is the bouldery **Smouldering Stirrups** E2 6a, The wider middle crack is the more sustained **Blazing Saddles** E2 5c. An easier variation, **Joas** VS 4c, moves right at the good jug and finishes up the wide hanging-crack.

On the west side of the valley is a large, clean slab, The Ghost Slab, to the left of it is a tall, vertical wall. On the left end of the wall is **Ripsnorter** E5 6a which climbs the left-facing corner beside the ash tree.

17 **The Ghost** E2 5b   23m

Wonderful, bold slab climbing. Climb up onto the slab and traverse left along the edge to the niche with difficulty. Follow the diagonal undercut and move right along the sloping ledge. Step up on small holds to the diagonal overlap. Climb this delicately and finish more easily up the shallow groove above. See photo on page 24.
S. Windrim, D. Windrim 11/07/1976

Haunted E5 6a starts as for The Ghost but follows the edge of the slab to the top. To the left of The Ghost two cracks run the full height of the slab, the left one is **Yorkshire Pudding** S 4a, the right one is the frequently damp **Honeypot Crack** S 3c.

18 **Masochist** E3 6a
20m

The thin crack right of Honeypot Crack. Follow the crack with increasing difficulty, with the crux being the moves just before the ledge. Finish more easily.
G. Jones, B. Walsh 01/06/1967
FFA H. Hebblethwaite April 1986

To the right is **Space Shuttle** E3 6b, which starts 4m left of the corner. Technical, unprotected slab climbing leads to a small horizontal edge, finish easily up the corner on the right.

The blocky wall right of the Ghost slab gets good sun and dries quickly. Its best routes follow a series of grooves up the left side of the wall.

19 **Stereo-Tentacles** HVS 5a
14m

Precarious, technical climbing. Scramble up to a sloping ledge below a vertical borehole. Follow the slabby corner on the left to a small ledge and peg at the base of another corner. Bridge up the corner and reach left to good holds. Finish easily.
S. Young, D. O'Murchu 28/07/1973

A worthwhile variation **Fang** HVS 5a climbs the slabby corner left of Stereo and traverses right under the roof joining Stereo on the small ledge below the crux but finishes right rather than left.

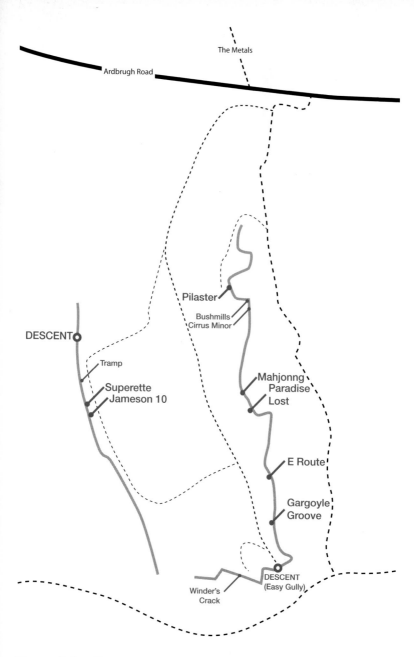

The Metals

Ardbrugh Road

Pilaster

Bushmills
Cirrus Minor

DESCENT

Tramp

Superette
Jameson 10

Mahjonng
Paradise
Lost

E Route

Gargoyle
Groove

DESCENT
(Easy Gully)

Winder's
Crack

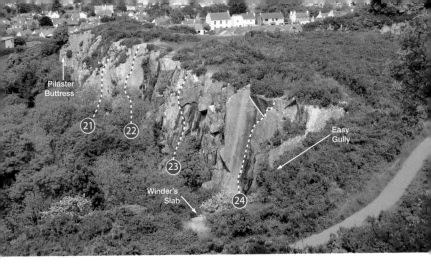

WEST VALLEY

Access the West Valley by the path at the mouth, by the narrow path beside Pilaster Buttress or **Easy Gully** D at the head of the quarry.

20 **Pilaster** VS 4c · 15m

A bold start leads to pleasant climbing. Follow a series of edges up the centre of the wall to a ledge. Continue more easily up the centre of the buttress and belay in the niche just below the top.
F. Maguire, A. Kopczynski 1951

There is a variation of Pilaster, that is similar in style but a little harder, **Crash Landing** E1 5c starts just to the right and traverses delicately right before a long reach from a flake gains the ledge. Finish as for Pilaster.

The next corner to the right is **Bushmills** E1 5b. **Cirrus Minor** E1 5b takes a protection-free weaving line up the slab to the right of Bushmills and **Bracket Wall** HVS 5a boldy climbs the groove right of the slab.

21 **Mahjongg** VS 4c · 12m

The thin crack that splits the centre of the slab is sustained and well protected. The diagonal crack to the right is **Levitation** HS 4b.
S. Young, J. Leonard, R. Richardson, M. Ryan, J. Butler 22/09/1973

22 **Paradise Lost** VD · 17m

Probably the most popular route in the quarry. Start in the middle of the slab and follow the cracks to a large flake. Make a committing and delicate step right from the top of the flake to a narrow crack which is followed to the top.
T. Calvert, W Perrott 1950

The stretch of blocky rock between Paradise Lost and Easy Gully has a range of moderate classics.

23 **E Route** VS 4b   24m

Start at the foot of the short wall at the flake. Make a thuggish move up the flake to the slab. Follow a crack up and left across the slab to the left end of the steep wall. Step left around the arete and up onto a small ledge. Make very delicate moves up the series of sloping ledges.
IMC Early 1940s

24 **Gargoyle Groove** HVS 5b   16m

Excellent climbing up the corner right of the slab (which is **The Green Fool** E5 6b). Pad up the easy angled slab to the foot of the corner. Make hard moves, on very polished rock to a ledge. Continue up the wall just right of the corner on small holds to the sharp arete and follow it right until it's possible to exit by an awkward mantel. A much better finish is to climb into the groove behind the sharp arete and traverse up and left **Gargoyle Groove Direct Finish** E1 5b.
P. O'Leary, S. Harmey 1957

Right of Easy Gully is a clean slab split by a crack. The left edge of the slab is the unfortunately often damp **Raspberry Ripple** VS 5a, the crack is **Winder's Crack** D, and the right arete is the bold **Paul's Edge** HVS 5a.

The following two routes tackle the headwall on the west side of the valley. Descend by walking along the path past the top of Tramp and climbing down the ramp on the right hand end of the cliff. It's also possible to abseil from the tree at the top of Jameson 10.

25 **Jameson 10** VS 4b   12m

Steep climbing on good holds. Start at the left end of the headwall and climb easily to the spike just below the overlap. Mantel onto the ledge (crux) above the overlap and follow the good holds up the right-hand of the two grooves for a few moves before stepping across to the left groove. Finish up this.
W. Dick 17/07/1966

26 **Superette** HVS 5a   12m

A good route up the right side of the headwall. Start 5m right of Jameson 10. Climb a series of sloping ledges and grooves to a ledge below the triangular niche. At the base of the niche follow the crack left and then up. A significantly easier version, **Delectissima** S, starts up the corner at the right end of the wall and finishes straight up the triangular niche.
FFA S. Young, D. O'Murchu 1974

The steep corner 8m right of Superette is taken by **Tramp** VS 4c, carry a big cam to protect the crux. The next corner to the right is **Dirty Dick** VS 4b.

FACING PAGE Leman Lemanski on Jameson 10 VS 4b. Photo by Seán Martin.

WICKLOW

The Wicklow Mountains are home to two superb multi-pitch granite crags, Glendalough and Luggala. Both have a good selection of classic routes but Glendalough is probably the more friendly of the two. However if you are looking for adventure then Luggala is the place to go.

Just south of Glendalough in the valley of Glenmalure is Great Gully Ridge, a great day out in the mountaineering vein.

ACCOMMODATION

The An Óige hostel in Glendalough www.anoige.ie (modern but a little pricey) and the Irish Mountaineering Club hut in Glendasan www.irishmountaineeringclub.org (good value and has a certain rustic charm) are both within walking distance of the crag in Glendalough. There are plenty of other options nearby including B+Bs, hotels and self-catering cottages, see www.visitwicklow.ie for some ideas.

Wild camping is permitted in Wicklow National Park but not allowed in the valley of Glendalough itself. There are also commercial campsites in Roundwood and Rathdrum.

OTHER CLIMBING

There are many other minor crags in Wicklow, the only one of note is Lough Dan, a steep granite crag with a range of high quality, hard, single-pitch routes. See www.climbing.ie for details.

Wicklow has the best and most extensive bouldering in Ireland (see page 19 for more information) with over 600 problems spread across more than a dozen areas.

REST/RAINY DAYS

Hiking and mountain biking are good options for rainy days. It can often be dry in Dalkey Quarry (see page 25) when it's damp in the hills and it's only a 45 minute drive from Glendalough. For rest days there are plenty of tourist attractions nearby and Dublin is only up the road.

FACING PAGE Rhys MacAillister on the first ascent of Just in Time E5 (5c,6a), Luggala. Photo by Stephen McGowan.

County Wicklow
LUGGALA
APPROACH **45 minutes**
ROCK **Granite**
D-S **1** - HS-HVS **5** - E1-E3 **9** - E4+ **1**

The massive mountain crag of Luggala has nearly 200, mostly multi-pitch routes, in a very picturesque setting above Lough Tay. In recent years it has been virtually ignored by the majority of climbers but it's a crag with huge potential that is well worth a visit.

The climbing is a little more subtle than in Glendalough, the holds are less positive and the route finding can be tricky as the routes tend to weave over and around obstacles rather then following very direct lines. A good selection of cams and double ropes are both pretty essential.

CONDITIONS

Luggala is prone to seepage and needs a few days to dry after rain. As it's relatively sheltered and gets the sun all day it can be very pleasant on sunny days in spring and autumn, however during the summer midges can be a problem.

DIRECTIONS

From Dublin head south on the M11. At Kilmacanoge turn left (signposted 'Glendalough') onto the R755. After 11km turn right onto the R759 (signposted 'Sallygap'). Continue straight through the crossroads and follow the road steeply uphill. Just after the crest of the hill where the cliffs come into view there is a stone wall and gate on the left. Park carefully on the verge opposite the gate. Don't leave any valuables in the car as this area is known for break-ins.

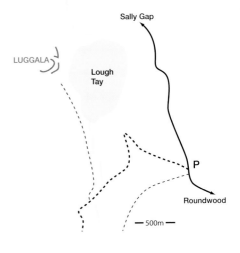

Follow the private road downhill (on foot - vehicles are not allowed) for 2km. Just beyond the bridge over the Cloghoge River cross the stile on the right and follow the river upstream. Pick up the path that skirts the lake shore and follow it to the foot of the scree. Scramble up through the boulders to the crag.

There is another, slightly quicker, approach over the boggy moorland plateau northwest of the crag, however it isn't the best option for the first time visitor.

WOODY WALL

The following route weaves its way up the steep wall that overlooks South Gully. To descend scramble to the top of the heather slopes and walk down South Gully.

1 All Along The Watchtower VS (4b,4a,4b)   62m

Exposed. Both leader and second need to be solid as the route features some committing traverses. Start at the right end of the grassy terrace.

P1   32m Climb the short corner right of the belay. Some awkward moves lead to the large sloping ledge (optional belay). Follow the narrow ramp left to a small ledge (see photo). Make a delicate move left to a wide crack which is followed to a dead tree. With help from the tree climb the steep wall above to the belay ledge.

P2   15m Exposed. Move down and right across the ramp with an airy step across a gap and a mantleshelf to a square-cut block. Continue across on better holds to a grassy ledge on the far side of the arete.

P3   15m Climb the clean groove, moving left to the arete at a bulge. Continue up and belay at the ledge.

K. Higgs, S. Windrim 19/04/1976

THIS PAGE Johnny Duignan on P1 of All Along the Watchtower VS (4b,4a,4b). Photo by Barry Denton.

Conifer Terrace

CONIFER BUTTRESS

Many of the routes on Conifer Buttress are heavily vegetated but the following routes which start from the left end of the Conifer Terrace are reasonably clean.

2 **No Quarter** E1 5b   30m

Bold and delicate. Start just left of the arete. Pull up onto a steep slab and make committing moves right to a vertical finger crack, use this to gain a ledge at the base of a clean-cut recess. Climb the left-hand wall via a ledge on the right to a small stance. Pull out right onto the face and follow a thin crack to a good foothold. Step up right and gain the arete (crux) which is followed to a tree belay. Abseil off.
R. Windrim 05/09/1976

3 **Man O'War** E3 5c   30m

Well protected, technical climbing. Start at a niche 2m left of the corner. Follow the diagonal crack until a metre below the arete. Step back right onto a foothold on the lip of the bulge (crux). Continue directly up the wall and belay in the trees. Abseil off.
D. O'Sullivan, T. Burke 08/06/1986

4 **Curved Air** VS (4b,4b)   77m

Enjoyable climbing in a fine situation. Start just over 30m along the Terrace at the undercut base of a clean leftward-trending groove.
P1   40m Climb over the small ledges on the right and move left to the base of the groove. Pass an awkward bulge at 5m and follow the groove to a large white ledge (optional belay). Climb the crack on the left and gain the slab above with difficulty. Move along a vegetated ramp to a short wall. Climb this on large holds and follow a heathery slab to the middle of an undercut wall on the right. Nut and peg belay.
P2   37m Climb the overlap using a jug, and traverse left to a wide crack in the middle of the wall. Follow this to a left-trending groove and crack, go up this with one awkward move. Follow a ramp diagonally left to the arete and belay at the gorse-covered ledge (belay requires #3 cam).
R. Windrim, K. Higgs 20/04/1976

SOUTH BUTTRESS

The left end of South Buttress features one worthwhile single-pitch route but the best climbing is further right where the crag is taller.

5 **Peregrine** E2 5c   30m

Steep and well protected. Start just left of a short corner with a holly tree. Climb the leftward slanting groove with difficulty to a ledge. From the ledge, climb up to another ledge below the headwall marked by quartz streaks. Traverse left around a nose to the steep hanging corner. This leads with increasing difficulty to the top.
C. Rice, D. Milnes June 1972
FFA S. Windrim 28/08/1977

Thriller

6

7

The next two routes tackle the steep ground in the middle of the buttress.

6 **Stepenwolf** E1 (5b,5b,3c)   70m

A high quality route, with a bold first pitch (bring very small nuts) and an exposed but well protected second pitch.
P1   25m Pull onto the slab and move up for 4m to a small spike on the right wall. Use this to gain a small ledge and climb up and slightly left to a difficult bulge which is followed on small holds to a left-trending ramp. Follow this to a belay at the tree.
P2   25m Move up a short slab on the left to the groove. Pull up using a sharp flake crack, step across right and climb the wall to the hanging block. Make delicate moves above the block onto the slab (crux) beneath the overhang. Climb the overhang on goods holds and follow a short groove to a narrow slab on the left. Up this to belay at the cracked blocks.
P3   20m Scrappy. Climb the cracked blocks to a heather ledge and then step right to the slab which leads to Conifer Terrace.
K. Higgs, S. Windrim, P. Ewen 16/04/1977

7 **Muskrat Ramble** HVS (5a,5a,4c)   75m

A fine climb at the top of the grade. The second pitch stands out, weaving it's way through steep, intimidating ground. Start on the right side of the slab just left of an overhanging wall.
P1   27m Climb the corner where the slab meets the steep wall on the right, it's harder than it looks from below. Move up and into a short corner and climb the groove above on the right to a grassy ledge. Traverse horizontally left to the oak tree.
P2   25m Climb the steep corner behind the tree. Move up the right-trending ramp. At the top of the ramp move up and slightly left to a short groove, after a move or two step right into another groove, climb this past a small holly tree to the foot of a short, vertical wall. Traverse left to belay at the tree.
P3   23m The final pitch of Crevasse Route is a better alternative than the original finish that takes the vegetated groove behind the tree. Move right from the tree to the foot of the steep bulge. Mantel over the bulge (crux) and step up and right to a crack, follow this up the slabby arete to belay on Conifer Terrace.
J. McKenzie, D. Blake 24/08/1975

The overhanging wall directly above the start of Muskrat is taken by the demanding **Thriller** E3 5c.

Left Side
Climb Direct

8

Further right along the foot of the crag is Pine Tree Buttress with its distinctive hanging slab.

8 Pine Tree Buttress S (3c,3c,3c,4a,4a)   87m

A classic route and very popular. The first and last pitches are a little scrappy but the crux pitch up the hanging slab more than makes up for them.

P1 12m Start 4m right of the holly tree. Climb the slab and move left to the large flake. Chimney up between the flake and the slab and belay on the ledge above.

P2 18m Traverse left around the corner into a groove. It's possible to reach this point directly from the ground avoiding the first pitch. At the top of the groove climb the wide crack on the left wall. Another short, easy crack leads to a belay at the holly tree.

P3 9m Step right onto the hanging wall and make a strenuous pull onto the ledge containing the small holly tree. Belay just above on the ledge at the foot of the corner that runs up the left side of the slab.

P4 35m Move up the corner in a wonderful exposed position. Follow the good holds towards the centre of the face, crossing a small overlap and trending up and right under the bugle to the heather ledge. Belay at the foot of the slabs. See photo above.

P5 13m Move up the slabs into a scoop below the overlap. Follow the crack through the overlap and belay at the pine tree.

J. Lynam, P. Crean 26/03/1949

An interesting, harder variation **Left Side Climb Direct** HVS (5b,4a,4c) tackles the series of corners left of the hanging slab.

Descend by walking to the left end of Conifer Terrace (passing below Woody Wall) and following the path along the base of the South Buttress back to the foot of the route. Or traverse right along Conifer Terrace and climb a route on the Main Face for a classic, long day's climbing.

ABOVE Gerry Moss on P4 of Pine Tree Buttress.

Clingon
Finish

THE MAIN FACE

Home to the steepest, cleanest rock on the crag. The taller right-hand side of the face features some long, hard routes while the left-hand side, above Conifer Ledge, has a few easier routes that sneak around either side of the Great Roof, the massive overhang at the top of the face.

The following climbs are found on the left side of the Main Face. They are best approached from Conifer Terrace.

9 **Clingon - Claidheamh Solais** VS (3c,4c,4b)   49m

A delightful combination of the best pitches of two routes. Start on Conifer Terrace directly below the Great Roof in a short corner beneath an overlap.
P1   13m Follow the easy slabs up and left. Belay just before the grassy ledge.
P2   20m Pull through the overlap (crux) above and just left of the belay. Climb the groove above and move left to the sloping belay ledge.
P3   16m The Claidheamh Solais pitch. Climb the slab directly above the belay to the overhang and move left and up to the roof and make a very committing step right onto the ledge. (Clingon continues left under the roof and finishes up the narrow chimney). Shuffle right and finish up the short groove, belay at the blocks.
Claidheamh Solais - T. Hand, J. McKenzie 01/05/1971
Clingon - C. Rice, P. Redmond 09/10/1971

10 **Spearhead** HVS (3c,4b,4a,5a)   62m

Straightforward, pleasant climbing leads to the spectacular crux.
P1   13m Follow P1 of Clingon.
P2   21m Step back down from the belay and make a long step right to a small sloping ledge. Move right and then up to the diagonal ramp which is followed to the short, steep corner.
P3   10m Climb the corner and traverse out right to belay in the corner beneath the Great Roof.
P4   18m Traverse right (plenty of exposure) and swing around the arete onto a slab and an awkward step up. Take care to ensure the rope doesn't get jammed. Finish easily up the slabs.
J. Deacon, V. Stephenson, F. Winder 10/08/1959

11 **The Gannets** E3 (4b,5c,5a)   85m

Exposed and strenuous climbing on very steep rock. Reasonable protection.
P1   25m Climb the slab to the left of the corner and move back right to the corner. Follow this until it steepens and eventually move out onto a sloping ledge.
P2   25m Descend from the belay to a ramp running left. Traverse this and climb the slab to a thin crack. Move up and right to the base of a clean-cut greenish corner (old peg). Climb the corner and move around the nose to a steep groove, go up this to good holds in a horizontal crack. Pull up to a small ledge on the arete to the right. Step right and climb the groove with difficulty to a large ledge on the right.
P3   35m Climb the detached block on the right and move off this to a slabby groove on the left. Continue up to a short overhanging corner until it's possible to swing out onto slabby rock on the right. Finish easily up this.
C. Rice, P. Redmond 18/04/1971
FFA K. Murphy, C. Torrans 21/05/1984

12 **Soyuz Ten** E3 (5c,5c)   70m

Another impressive and sensationally exposed climb taking the prominent hanging groove up the centre of the Main Face.

P1   30m Pull onto the slab and go up this to the overhang on the right. Climb this strenuously, pulling out right to a stance. Move up right and climb steeply to a wide crack in a flake. Traverse left to the arete, pull around this and move up to a small stance (peg and good nuts).

P2   40m Traverse right, either by following a low line or by a mantleshelf onto a higher ledge. Climb the steep wall and move up to a small slab below a hanging groove. Gain the groove with difficulty and climb it with further difficulty to reach better holds. Continue directly up and move slightly left at a horizontal flake. Go up easy slabs to a thread belay at a block.

S. Billane, P. McHugh June 1970
FFA R. Dean, T. Curtis 1982

The start of the next route is accessed by following the grassy slopes around from the base of the South Buttress.

13 **Banshee** E2 (5c,4a,5a,5a,4a)   135m

An incredible, devious line through the longest, most continuous section of rock on the crag.

P1   30m Climb the left-trending ramps and slabs to a grassy ledge. Move up a short steep corner on the right to a shoulder and step up to the right and then back left into a groove. Follow the groove with increasing difficulty to the overhang. Climb the overhang (crux) and continue up a short, shallow groove to a small stance with a nut and old peg belay.

P2   22m Follow a grassy crack and then traverse left for a few metres. Follow a crack up the slab to blocks below the overhanging wall. Traverse right across the blocks to belay at the large detached block.

P3   13m Climb onto the detached block and up the short wall on the right which is hard to start. Move up the slab above to a flake crack belay.

P4   30m A fine pitch which starts directly up the quartz rib below the overhang. Gain the overhang on good holds and make an awkward move left into a groove. Follow this to a resting place on the left. Traverse steeply right on large holds and move up the line of weakness to a heather groove. Continue up for 3m to belay on the slab below the overhanging wall.

P5   40m Traverse left across the slab to the base of the chimney. Climb this and pull out left onto slabs which are followed to the top.

C. Rice, D. Milnes June 1972
FFA K. Higgs, J. Colton May 1977

Stampede

North
Gully

16

14

15

NORTH BUTTRESS

The North Buttress is more prone to seepage than the Main Face and can be a little
vegetated but it's worth persevering with. Access the following routes by the North
Gully. If descending the gully from above be extremely careful as the top section of is
frequently wet and slippery.

14 Friends Laughing Alphabetically E4 (6a,6a)   95m

An entertaining variation on the original aid route with two contrasting pitches, the
first is steep and the second serious.

P1   50m Climb up the corner to a stance below the big roof. Traverse left across
the steep wall (crux) to an overhanging arete and swing wildly upwards on big holds
to the lip and slab above. Clamber up the grass terrace, to a block belay.

P2   45m Follow the slab to the centre of the roof which is breached on improving
holds (crux). An awkward traverse left under the second roof leads to a third roof.
Make a gripping traverse right under this roof to a blobby slab. Climb this trending
slightly left to finish up a grass gully.

S. Young and party 1980
FFA R. Browner, H. Hebblethwaite 16/07/2013

15 Dance of the Tumblers E1 (5b,5a)   55m

A superb route following an intricate and exposed line.

P1   30m Climb the left trending slab and follow the curving green slab to a short
corner. Step up and move steeply left to a rest. Pull up to a small ledge below an
overlap. Move left to a large hold on the arete and swing onto the sloping ledge
above. Make a delicate and exposed slightly descending traverse right below the
overhang until a step down leads to better footholds. Continue right to a ledge.
Climb up onto the slab above to a flake crack to belay.

P2   25m Move slightly left for 3m and pull over a small bulge. Continue steeply
on good sidepulls to a groove on the right. Follow this to a sloping ledge below
the overhanging chimney. Climb this (thread runner) and exit with difficulty to a
spectacular position and a large spike hold high on the left. Continue more easily to a
block belay on the terrace.

S. Young, J. Mulhall, R. Richardson, M. Harris 16/07/1972
FFA D. Richardson 1973

16 Official E2 (4b,5b)   45m

Strenuous climbing up the imposing crack on the upper wall. **Stampede** VS (4b,4c)
offers an easier alternative.

P1   25m Climb the slab out to the left to a crack. Follow this to shattered green
rock and traverse right treating the rock with care to a large grassy ledge.

P2   20m Climb straight up for 4m and then move left to the base of a steep crack.
Follow this with increasing difficulty (crux) to where it widens to a chimney. Finish
more easily up this.

C. Rice, D. Milnes September 1971
FFA S. Windrim, D. Windrim 22/08/1976

County Wicklow

GLENDALOUGH
APPROACH **50 minutes**
ROCK **Granite**
D-S **1** - HS-HVS **16** - E1-E3 **6** - E4+ **1**

This popular crag lies at the head of the Glendalough Valley, high up on the hillside. It boasts a wonderful selection of quality routes, particularly in the HS-HVS range, with well-protected climbing, clean rough granite and great scenery.

CONDITIONS

The crag is exposed to the wind, a blessing during the summer as there is usually a breeze to keep the midges at bay. It's south facing so it can be quite pleasant on calm, sunny winter days.

DIRECTIONS

From Dublin head south on the M11. At Kilmacanoge turn left onto the R755 (signposted 'Glendalough') and pass through the villages of Roundwood and Laragh. Follow the road past the hotel in Glendalough and park in the (paying) carpark beside the Upper Lake.

From the carpark follow the track along the north side of the Upper Lake. Pass through the Miner's Village and follow the track past the boulders. Near the head of the valley the track steepens and starts to switchback, leave the track at the fourth hairpin bend and follow a vague, steep path up through the scree to the crag.

FACING PAGE An unknown climber on the final moves of P3 of Prelude-Nightmare VS (4b,4a,4c) (see page 65).

Upper Cliffs

Anchor

Stray Dog

①

②

③

FAR WEST BUTTRESS

The series of corners and slabs left of the Main Face is quite sheltered and gets the sun late in the day.

To get there follow the main path up through the scree, and continue straight up aiming for the left arete of the Main Face, ignoring the paths that branch off to the right to the foot of the Main Face. Just before the Buttress there are a few tricky rock steps that require care.

Descend from the in-situ anchor at the top of the Expectancy Slab using one 50m rope.

1 **Cracks on the Garden of Eden** HVS 5a	38m

Historically climbed in two or even three wandering pitches but the modern approach is to do it in one long pitch, attacking the difficulties head on rather than skirting around them. Start at a short right-facing corner 20m above and left of the Expectancy Slab. Climb the corner to a small sloping ledge. Follow the finger crack directly above through the steep bulge. The crack widens and leads more easily to a ledge (optional belay) below the steep headwall. Finish up this wall following the pumpy crack/groove line. An easier variation at VS (4c,4c) moves right after the initial corner, belays at the tree and finishes up the headwall.
Lower section - J. Morrison 1951
Upper section - R. Ohrtmann 08/03/1953

The right arete of the middle slab is taken by **Stray Dog** E1 5b. The slab on the right, Expectancy Slab, is home to a half dozen routes, notably the eponymous Expectancy.

2 **Expectancy** VD 3c	21m

A beautiful clean line that follows the right-facing corner that runs up the middle of the slab. Halfway up the generous holds disappear, but after a few layback moves up the corner and a step left onto the face they reappear and it's an easy romp to the anchor.
F. Maguire, A. Kopczynski, S. Rothery 20/04/1952

3 **Deirdre** VS 4c	25m

A testing route that tackles the left edge of the Main Face. Start 2m right of the arete and follow the shallow corner to the ledge. The thin crack above leads to the left end of the heather ledge. Climb the arete for a few moves until it's possible to traverse left around the arete using the horizontal crack. Make bold but steady moves directly up the slab to regain the arete and finish easily to belay at the anchor. An easier variation steps right from the first ledge to another crack that leads to the right side of the heather ledge and finishes easily up the wide crack.
F. Winder, P. Kelly 07/06/1953

THE MAIN FACE

The clean steep slab is the focal point of the crag thanks to its collection of amenable classics. It catches the sun and dries quickly. It's possible to mix and match pitches from various routes, Spillikin - Fanfare - Nightmare is one very popular permutation but there are plenty of others.

To access the routes between Quartz Gully and Sarcophagus traverse right across a heather ledge from the main path once you are about level with the foot of the face.

Descend by abseiling (two 60m ropes required) from the in-situ anchor at the top of Prelude-Nightmare. If you only have one rope walk around to the top of the Expectancy Slab and abseil using the in-situ anchor.

4 **Quartz Gully** HS (3c,4b) 52m

A wonderful route with an exposed but well protected crux.
P1   12m A little scrappy. Follow broken vegetated ground to the start of the quartz vein and belay at the block.
P2   40m Tricky moves leaving the belay lead to good quartz holds that are followed through a narrowing. Move left across the sloping ledge to the diagonal crack. Follow the crack on good hand holds and smears (crux) to regain the vein. Back and foot through the chimney to a large ledge (optional belay). Finish up the corner to the right of the thin, leaning block.
F. Winder, P. Kenny 06/08/1950

5 **Prelude-Nightmare** VS (4b,4a,4c) 74m

A classic route up the middle of the face. See photo on page 56.
P1   34m Start just right of the small, shallow cave and carefully pad left across the sloping ledge. Move up and left across the clean slab to a small ledge. Bridge up the recess above until it's possible to pull left using holds on the horizontal break. Continue directly up on good holds to belay at the large flake.
P2   16m Traverse left for two metres to the base of the left-facing corner. Follow this and the cracks above until nearly level with the sensational Nightmare Ledge at which point you traverse right to the ledge. Peg and nut belay.
P3   24m Make a few moves up the steep crack at the back of the ledge before stepping right onto the slab and making a long stride right to the steep quartz crack. Follow the crack and move right on big holds to the arete for the last few moves. Belay at the anchor.
F. Winder, B. Healy June 1953

6 **Spéirbhean** VS 4c 20m

Hard for the grade but with plenty of character. Traverse left from Nightmare Ledge to the foot of a groove just right of the arete. Follow the groove to the slab. Boldly climb the slab for a few moves before stepping left to the arete which is followed to the top.
S. Rothery, B. McCall 15/04/1956

7 **Scimitar Crack** HVS 5a 40m

Excellent climbing up the middle of the face. Start from the belay at the top of the first pitch of Prelude-Nightmare. Follow the quartz vein up and right with increasing difficulty. After the steep crux the difficulty and the angle ease. Finish as for Prelude-Nightmare.
F. Winder, S. Rothery 28/06/1953

FACING PAGE Kevin Kilroy on P2 of Sarcophagus HVS (5a,5a,5a) (see page 67).

Anchor

Left
Wall
Crack

6

Nightmare
Ledge

Bathsheba

9

Spillikin
Ledge

7

10

5

8

8 **Spillikin Ridge** E3 (4c,5c)   85m

A much sought-after hard classic. The large pillar - the Spillikin - is long departed and left in its place a significantly harder route.

P1   43m Climb the shallow quartz groove on good holds. Move left to a ledge and continue directly up via a thin crack and small groove to Spillikin Ledge.

P2   42m Climb the shallow groove directly above the belay to the first bulge. Overcome this (crux) and continue up the crack with difficulty to a second, slightly easier, bulge. A wide crack leads to the third overhang. Traverse left on jugs to join Scimitar Crack for a few moves before moving back right where a balancy move leads to the final arete.

F. Winder, P. Kenny, P. Hill, S. Rothery 13/06/1954
FFA C. Torrans, S. Darby October 1980

9 **Fanfare** VS 4c   20m

An interesting pitch that links Spillikin Ledge and Nightmare Ledge. Follow the first pitch of Spillikin Ridge (which is VS) to Spillikin Ledge. From the ledge descend slightly left and make a memorable step around the arete to a short wall. Step up delicately and move diagonally left, crossing the quartz vein of Scimitar, heading for Nightmare Ledge. Finish up the last pitch of Prelude-Nightmare or Spéirbhean.

F. Winder, P. Kenny 07/06/1953

10 **Sarcophagus** HVS (5a,5a,5a)   84m

Sustained but well protected bridging up the series of corners right of Spillikin Ridge. High in the grade. The second and third pitches can be combined but most leaders will welcome the chance to rest and regroup after the crux. See photo on page 64.

P1   36m Start up the first pitch of Spillikin Ridge. After about 20m move right, passing a pair of parallel cracks, to a small ledge (optional belay). Climb the tricky corner above to belay at the holly tree.

P2   32m The crux pitch. Bridge up the corner, the hardest moves are early on but it doesn't really let up. Gain the arete and move up the wide crack, belaying just above on the ledge.

P3   16m Climb the steep corner. An interesting and sustained variation **Left Wall Crack** E1 (5b,5b) breaks out from the belay across the wall to the right and finishes up the overhanging crack on the other side of the arete.

E. Goulding, A. Ingram 27/05/1961

The clean wall left of the second pitch of Sarcophagus is taken by **Bathsheba** E5 6b.

Forest Wall

Forest Ledge

Great North Road

Shanghai Corner

13

11

12

Acorn Buttress

Provo

Facilis Descensus

ACORN BUTTRESS

The small crag is popular with groups and beginners and is a good spot to squeeze in one more quick route. **Provo** VS 4c and **Facilis Descensus** HS 4b are both worthwhile.

EAST WING

The East Wing is the area of rock right of the waterfall, directly above Acorn Buttress. Descend by abseil from the in-situ anchor at the top of Forest Wall to Forest Ledge, then scramble down through the trees and abseil from the top of the first pitch of Forest Rhapsody.

11 **Forest Rhapsody** VS (4c,-,4a,4b)   110m

The lower pitches of this popular classic form the approach to Forest Ledge.
P1   52m Climb the left hand side of the arete with a few tricky moves near the top. Cross the notch (optional belay) which can also be reached by scrambling up from the left. Move up the slab on the left and follow the quartz groove on good holds to a belay near the start of the thick undergrowth.
P2   15m Scramble easily up through the trees to Forest Ledge. Belay at the large block at the left end of the ledge.
P3   21m Step right off the block onto a ledge, move right across this and make a delicate move across the sloping ledge to a small corner. Follow the corner and the wide crack above to the large ledge.
P4   22m Climb over the series of ledges at the back of the corner, moving closer to the steep left wall as you gain height. Finish up the short slab.
S. Rothery, F. Winder 26/10/1952

The next two routes are on the steep, clean slab. They can be linked with **Great North Road** E3 (5c,4c) or **Shanghai Corner** E3 (5c,4a) on the wall above.

12 **Setanta** E1 5b   33m

A long and varied pitch. Start up the pillar at the foot of the slab. From the top of the pillar step across and up to a grassy ledge. Move diagonally right up the thin quartz vein and follow it to a bulge (old peg). Pull directly up a thin crack to a narrow ledge. Step right to the arete and finish more easily. Belay at the tree and abseil off (two 60m ropes required).
P. O'Halpin, E. Healy 29/04/1962
FFA S. Windrim, D. Windrim 1974

13 **Graceland** E3 6a   33m

Nice, well protected climbing. Follow Setanta to the bulge. Climb the left-hand crack until it's possible to reach a good flake on the left. Mantel onto the flake, step left and follow the broken cracks to the top. Belay at the tree and abseil off (two 60m ropes required).
H. Hebblethwaite May 1988

FOREST WALL

Forest Wall is home to an array of great VSs. Approach via Forest Rhapsody.
Descend by abseiling from the in-situ anchor at the top of Forest Wall to Forest
Ledge, then scrambling down through the trees and abseiling from the top of the first
pitch of Forest Rhapsody.

14 Jackey VS 4c   29m

Belay at the left arete of Forest Wall and move left around the arete to the base of the
triangular slab. Follow the arcing left-hand crack on generous holds to a ledge. Climb
the corner above and belay at the anchor.
P. Higgins, E. Gaffney March 1963
FFA E. Goulding 1963

15 Celia VS 4c   29m

Start as for Jackey but climb the right-hand crack. Near the top step right to the
arete and climb easily to the ledge, finish up the corner as for Jackey.
E. Goulding, P. Higgins, E. Gaffney March 1963

16 Aisling Arete VS 4c   28m

The wide crack just right of the arete has a bold start but is well-protected after that.
Follow the crack to the ledge and finish as for Jackey.
P. Kenny, B. Moss 08/03/1953
Direct start off Forest Ledge - P. Kenny, J. McKenzie 1971

17 Concrete Wallflower E1 5b   28m

The thin crack just right of Aisling Arete. Follow the thin crack up the steep slab,
delicate moves gain a ledge. Continue through the steepness above via a few easier
but strenuous pulls. See photo on page 72.
K. Higgs June 1977

18 Lethe VS 4c   31m

Start from the large block. Follow the quartz crack until it's possible to step left into
the groove (**Lethe Direct** HVS 5b takes the right hand groove) follow this for a few
moves and escape left before heading directly up to the anchor.
P. Kenny, F. Winder, S. Rothery 25/04/1954
FFA P. O'Leary 1972

19 Ifreann Direct HVS (5b,5b)   33m

Superb finger jamming. Start below the prominent, rectangular roof.
P1 18m Climb the splitter crack passing the right side of the roof to belay at the
holly tree.
P2 15m Take the short, clean, square-cut chimney and belay at the top of P3 of
Forest Rhapsody.
E. Goulding, J. Tobin, S. Rothery, P. Kavanagh 06/03/1966

UPPER CLIFFS

Most of the routes on the Upper Cliffs are rambling and heavily vegetated but there are a few worthwhile routes however they require a good spell of dry weather before they come into condition.

20 **Silent Movie** E3 (5c,5c) 67m Might need a brush.
21 **Lifeline** E4 (6a, 5b) 30m Very bold slab climbing on pristine granite.
22 **Cornish Rhapsody** E1 (5a,5b) 56m "A minor masterpiece".
23 **Freebird** HVS (5a,4c) 38m The vegetated crack on the left side of the slab.
24 **Cúchulainn Groove** VS (4a,4c) 45m The prominent corner, never fully dries.

FACING PAGE An unknown climber on Concrete Wallflower E1 5b (see page 71). Photo by Richard Creagh.

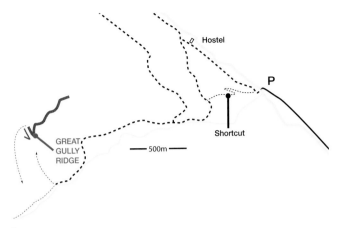

County Wicklow

GLENMALURE
APPROACH **60 minutes**
ROCK **Granite**
D-S **0** - HS-HVS **1** - E1-E3 **0** - E4+ **0**

Great Gully Ridge is an adventurous multi-pitch route that follows the prominent ridge on the south wall of Fraughan Rock Glen in Glenmalure. The climbing is always interesting, on clean rock and is well protected.

CONDITIONS

The ridge's relatively high altitude and exposed setting mean that, outside of the summer months, it can get cold. But this also means that in the summer midges are rarely a problem and the rock dries quickly.

DIRECTIONS

Follow the directions on page 57 as far as Laragh. In the village turn left at Lynam's Pub, follow the road and turn right (signposted 'Glenmalure') shortly after you cross the narrow bridge. Continue for 8km to the crossroads at Glenmalure Lodge where you turn right and park in the large carpark at the end of the road.

Cross the Avonbeg River at the footbridge just upstream of the carpark and follow the main track past the hostel, turning left at the junction (there is a good shortcut up a narrow path that starts directly opposite the footbridge but it can be hard to find). Follow the track into the Fraughan Rock Glen, at the head of the valley, shortly after the track becomes narrower and steeper, break out right across rough ground and bushwack up to the foot of the ridge. Alternatively walk to the top of the ridge and abseil down to the start.

FACING PAGE Theo Mooney at the belay at the top of P4.

Everyone seems to climb the route slightly differently so the following description is just one suggested approach.

Great Gully Ridge HS (4a,3b,4b,3b,4a)   140m

Start at the foot of the ridge at the corner.

P1   10m Climb the corner - tricky start - to a wide crack. Belay on the heather ledge under the overhang at the top of the crack.

P2   45m Follow the ridge, scrambling over a series of easy steps. Belay beneath the large flat stone that sits on the crest of the ridge.

P3   25m Climb the crack that splits the slab (crux). Belay at the block just before the heather ledge.

P4   30m A few easy steps lead to a large boulder perched on the ledge, just past this, on the left side of the ridge, is an in-situ thread. Pass the thread and follow broken ground to the base of the vertical wall that is split by a thin crack. Mantel onto the rock ledge on the left and cross this before stepping left and down to a heather ledge at the foot of a corner. Belay here (see photo on page 74).

P5   30m Climb the corner above, passing a peg. Finish up and slightly right to belay at the chain. A slightly harder, more direct alternative (VS 5a) climbs the wall to the right.

J. Morrison, A. Kopczynski 1951

The quickest descend is to walk south across the heather slopes to the path that leads back into Fraughan Glen. It's also possible to abseil but this means retracing your steps down the steep, vegetated approach slopes. Abseiling from the chain at the top of the route with two 50m ropes will (just) get you to the lower part of the gully.

ABOVE Looking down at the ridge from the top of the gully.

County Waterford

COUMSHINGAUN

APPROACH **45 minutes**
ROCK **Conglomerate**
D-S **0** - HS-HVS **6** - E1-E3 **8** - E4+ **3**

Coumshingaun, one of the most spectacular corries in Europe, is ringed with cliffs of rough conglomerate. The impressive east wall is home to a handful of hard adventure climbs. The south wall, while well positioned suffers from less than prefect rock. It's on the north facing crag where the best climbing is to be found.

On first impression the rock doesn't look inspiring but it's actually quite clean and interesting to climb. The routes are steep, most follow cracks and corners and are well protected. Two 50m ropes are required for the abseil descents.

CONDITIONS

In general, being north facing, the crag doesn't get much sun, however the west end gets the sun on summer evenings. Seepage is rarely a problem but as with all north facing cliffs it requires some wind to dry after rain or heavy dew.

DIRECTIONS

Pass south through Carrick-on-Suir onto the R676, after 15km you will see a carpark on the right (signposted 'Kilclooney Wood'). Park here. Coming from Dungarvan head north on the N25, after 12km turn left onto the R676.

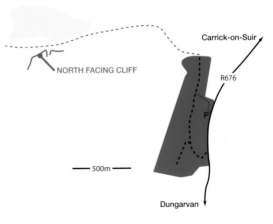

From the carpark take the path that leads up through the trees, when you meet the main track turn right and follow it to the edge of the forest. Cross the fence and follow the path up along the edge of the forest, at the corner head up and right on vague paths, towards the rounded ridge on the skyline. From the ridge follow one of the many paths that lead across the hillside into the corrie. Follow the high path above the southern shore of the lake to the crag.

FACING PAGE Dave Cussen on P2 of Controlled Burning E3 (4b,5c) (see page 85).

MAIN GULLY

The following route climbs the vertical wall on the west side of the Main Gully.

1 **The Sleep of Reason** E4 6a   35m

An athletic route with sustained difficulty and interest. Climb the arete to the diagonal cracks which are followed left as far as the overlap. Briefly traverse right before moving straight up and getting established above the overlap (crux). Climb diagonally right, joining the arete at a spike. Follow the arete easily to the overhang which is climbed on the left of the arete. **The Sleep of Reason Direct** E5 6a follows the arete all the way to the final overhang.
S. Gallwey 07/05/1989
Direct - H. Fogg, G. Fogg 2009

EMPEROR BUTTRESS

2 **Kishon** HVS 5a   50m

An easy but bold start leads to sustained, well protected climbing. Chimney up the edge of the detached flake. At the ledge, move left from the corner and climb the short hanging slab and the thin crack which leads to the corner above and thence to the higher corner above and to the left. Finish up the short vertical wall with good gear. With 50m ropes, it is necessary to belay above this and let your second lead through the last few metres to the ledge. Abseil descent.
G. Fogg, H. Fogg 15/05/2010

3 **Prophets of Baal** E1 5b   48m

Start as for Kishon. From the ledge climb the corner to the right and breach the overhang. Climb the higher, wider overhang and niche above. Continue on to the ledge. Abseil descent.
G. Fogg H. Fogg 15/05/2010

Anchor

⑥

Higher belay for Talking God

③

Direct
Start

④ ⑤

②

EMPEROR WEST FACE

Descend by walking directly up the hill until it's possible to traverse off to the east along sheep tracks into the Main Gully which is followed down to the foot of the crag.

4 **Emperor's Nose** E2 (5b,5b)   60m

A stunning line. The crux on the first pitch must be one of the best moves in Irish climbing. The start is hard but the holds improve after a few moves. Access the start by traversing left around the arete.
P1   27m Start below the corner, just left of a square-cut overhang at 4m. Move up the wall to the ledge at 5m. Climb the corner until the crack in the back of it closes at 15m. With difficulty reach a large hold on the arete to the right. Swing out and mantleshelf it (crux). Continue up the arete to a ledge. Step back left into the corner and move up easy ground to belay at the back of the grassy ledge. Avoid the loose flake.
P2   33m Well protected by large cams (up to #4). Follow the good crack past the nose and belay on the ledge on the right just below the top.
S. Gallwey, W. Lee August 1980

5 **Dark Angel** HVS (5a,5a)   60m

Majestic corner climbing. Don't be put off by its green appearance, it's one of the best and most popular routes in the coum.
P1   25m Start just left of the arete and climb the crack, move left where it steepens and follow the flakes to a sloping ledge below the roof.
P2   35m Move right into the corner and follow it to the top. The crux is passing the first overlap.
O. Jacob, S. Gallwey June 1980

6 **Talking God** E5 (4c,6a)   59m

Exciting, exposed, well protected climbing up right arete of the Emperor Buttress.
P1   29m Climb the first pitch of Dark Angel, and continue for 4m to belay on a small stance level with the first of the two overhangs on the left.
P2   30m Move left out of the corner, just above the overhangs, to a crack which is climbed with sustained difficulty until it's possible to reach the arete below the overhanging section for a good rest. Climb the overhanging arete on large holds to the nose which is passed on its right side. Reach back left to the arete and follow it more easily to the top. It's possible start this pitch more directly, climbing straight up through the overhangs from the Dark Angel belay at E6 6a.
S. Gallwey, J. Bergin July 1991
P2 direct - H. Fogg 22/06/2014

Anchor

9 10

11

8

Black
Chocolate
Gully

7

ATOM ANT WALL

This clean, vertical wall has the largest concentration of high quality, hard routes in the coum. Descend by abseil from the bolts at the top of the wall.

7 **Crooked Smile** HVS (4b,5a)   60m

This climb takes the crooked chimney/corner system which splits the arete.
P1   20m Start from the ledge just left of the arete. Climb the flakes on the arete and then up the right-hand wall. Traverse right to a crack splitting a large block. From the top of block, step across to a ledge and belay at the base of the short corner.
P2   40m Climb the corner and traverse left to the foot of the chimney. Follow the chimney to the hanging slab. Climb the slab until forced out onto the arete by the overhang. Pass the overhang on its left and finish up the hanging slab.
E. Hernstadt, S. Gallwey June 1981

8 **Tyger Tyger** E3 (4b,5c)   55m

The superb finger crack.
P1   20m As for P1 of Crooked Smile.
P2   35m Climb the left side of the large flake that leans against the face. Follow the crack to the last few metres of Crooked Smile.
S. Gallwey, J. Bergin April 1988

9 **Grendel** E1 (4b,5b)   60m

The steep corner just right of Tyger Tyger.
P1   20m As for P1 of Crooked Smile.
P2   40m Climb the flake as for Tyger Tyger and step right to the base of the corner. Climb the corner, turn the overhang on its right (crux) and finish up the short corner above.
E. Hernstadt, S. Gallwey August 1984

10 **Atom Ant** E2 (4b,5c)   40m

This strenuous route takes a diagonal line up the wall right of Grendel.
P1   20m As for P1 of Crooked Smile.
P2   Follow Grendel to the base of the corner and climb the diagonal crack to a small ledge. Finish directly up the wall above as for Controlled Burning.
S. Gallwey, E. Hernstad August 1984
Direct finish - S. Gallwey, J. Bergin. June 1991

11 **Controlled Burning** E3 (4b,5c)   50m

Climbs the thin crack on the right side of the wall.
P1   20m As for P1 of Crooked Smile. Belay to the right of the flake.
P2   30m Move up the vegetated ledge to the thin crack. After a tricky start the holds and protection improve. Follow the crack to a ledge and finish directly up the wall above. See photo on page 78.
S. Gallwey, J. Bergin May 1991

BLACK CHOCOLATE GULLY

The following routes start from the upper reaches of the west side of the deep gully. Beware of falling down behind the large chockstone.

12 Colours on the Water E3 5c   40m

Start at the prominent crack on the right hand wall. Climb the crack past a large horizontal break and continue to easier ground just below the top of the wall. Abseil from the bolts that are to the right, just below the top.
G. Fogg, S. Gallwey 17/06/2006

13 **Satanic Majesty** E3/4 6a   40m

Follow Colours on the Water to the horizontal break and traverse right to a loose pedestal. Hard moves above this gain the main crack system which is followed to the overhang. Traverse right under overhang and finish up the easy corner. Abseil descent.
S. Gallwey, G. Fogg August 2001

14 **Filamingo** HVS 5a   45m

A sustained and continuously interesting climb, very popular. Start at the foot of the prominent corner directly opposite Atom Ant Wall. Climb the corner to an airy pulpit. Abseil descent from bolts.
P. Britton, C. Ennis, H. Fogg, N. Walls 13/06/2004

THE WEST END

The series of ribs at the western end of the crag has a pleasant open feel and gets more light than the routes to the east. Descend down the grassy slopes further to the west.

15 **Ansty's Desire** HVS (4b,5a)   75m

The very enjoyable, airy arete.
P1   30m Layback up the broken corner until it's possible to step left onto the slab. Continue up the slab and follow the offwidth crack on the right to a grassy ledge. Climb another offwidth crack spectacularly to a large pulpit and belay.
P2   45m Traverse left onto the arete on large holds and climb to the top.
J. Bergin, S. Gallwey 03/06/1991

16 **Perpetual Motion** E1 (4c,5b,4c)   75m

Good climbing.
P1   20m Climb the corner on good holds. Break onto the face at the overhang and continue up to belay on a small ledge on the face.
P2   20m Climb the crack with increasing difficulty. Surmount the overhang on small holds and move up to the base of the next, larger overhang. Traverse delicately to the left and continue up to belay on the arete.
P3   35m As for P2 of A Walk On The West End.
J. Bergin. S. Gallwey 23/05/1991

17 **A Walk On The West End** HS (4c,4c)   70m

One of the best easier routes at the crag. The start is a little scrappy but the climbing improves with height.
P1   35m Start up the slab and move left to the arete and follow it to a large belay ledge.
P2   35m Climb the arete to the top. The first few moves are the crux.
J. Bergin, S. Gallwey 16/05/1991

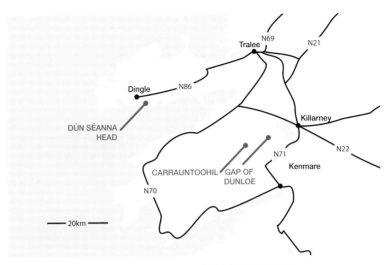

KERRY

Surprisingly the mountains and coast of Kerry contain relatively few climbing areas, however the three areas included here are all excellent and offer a good variety of climbing.

ACCOMMODATION

The busy tourist town of Killarney is only a short drive from the Gap of Dunloe and Carrauntoohil. It offers the full range of accommodation from camp sites, hostels and B+Bs to hotels.

Cronin's Yard in Beaufort, at the trailhead for Carrauntoohil, has parking, camping and a tea rooms www.croninsyard.com.

The town of Dingle is only a few minutes drive from Dún Séanna Head and has a few decent hostels and plenty of pubs.

OTHER CLIMBING

Some very impressive, hard routes have been climbed on the sea cliffs of the Dingle and Iveragh peninsulas, consult www.climbing.ie for more information.

There is some good bouldering in the Gap and in the nearby Black Valley (see *Bouldering in Ireland* for details).

REST/RAINY DAYS

There is plenty of wonderful scrambling and hiking in the mountains of Kerry. Routes such as Faha Ridge on Brandon, and Stumpa an tSaimh in the Reeks are quality scrambles ideal for days when it's too damp to climb (see *The Ridges of England, Wales and Ireland* for details). Mightn't be much of a rest day though.

The only climbing wall in Kerry is Play at Height just outside Dingle Town.

FACING PAGE Michael Reardon on The Stoop E2 5c, Gap of Dunloe (see page 107). Photo by Damon Corso.

County Kerry

CARRAUNTOOHIL

APPROACH **120 minutes**
ROCK **Sandstone**
D-S **1** - HS-HVS **0** - E1-E3 **0** - E4+ **0**

Howling Ridge is the classic Irish mountaineering route. The long continuous ridge runs up the centre of the northeast face of Ireland's highest peak, Carrauntoohil, finishing just below the summit. It offers 300 metres of easy but interesting climbing with massive exposure and amazing views (on the rare days that it's clear).

However don't be fooled by Howling's low grade and popularity, yes on a warm summer's day it's an easy romp but it can feel very different in the rain, dark and cold. Over the years the worst of the loose rock has been cleared but the rock still needs be treated with caution and every hold tested. Bear in mind that any dislodged material will fall onto the Heavenly Gates path below.

Most parties climb Howling in big boots, moving together and pitching where appropriate. It's advisable to keep pitches short to minimise rope drag and reduce the chances of the rope dislodging any rock. Carry plenty of long slings for running belays rather then placing small nuts which can be unreliable in the loose rock. A map, compass and good navigation skills are vital as the Macgillycuddy's Reeks are a large, complex mountain range and frequently shrouded in cloud and mist.

The ridges to the left (**Pipit Ridge** S) and the right (**Primroses** HVS) offer harder, looser alternatives but won't be to most people's taste.

CONDITIONS

Even though Howling was first climbed in winter conditions nowadays it's more commonly done as a scramble/easy rock climb. It is frequently climbed in wet conditions however it should be avoided in strong winds.

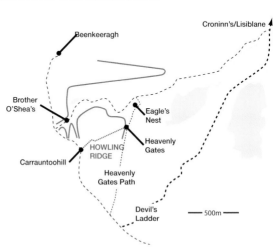

FACING PAGE Denis Dineen climbing Howling on a typical 'soft day'. Photo by Richard Creagh.

DIRECTIONS

From Killarney take the N72 west. After 6km turn left (signposted 'Gap of Dunloe') and follow the road. After 8km there is a turn left for Cronin's Yard, a paying carpark with a cafe and showers. Either take this or continue for another 1.5km, turn left and drive to the end of the road, keeping right at the junction, to the (free) carpark.

From the carpark take the wide flat track up the Hag's Glen. After 2km, just before the track fords the Gaddagh River, branch right following a vague path alongside the stream that drains the lough. Follow the path as it makes a rising traverse up the rocky slopes passing a few easy scrambling steps as far as the lowest level of the hanging valley. Here you branch left and climb the spur known as Eagle's Nest. Pass the Emergency Hut at the top of the spur and follow the loose path along the foot of the cliff to the notch on the left skyline, this is Heavenly Gates (GR V 807 844).

THIS PAGE David Flanagan passing the easy pinnacles above The Bridge. Photo by Peter McMahon.

The Bridge

The Tower

Collins' Gully

Pipit Ridge

Primroses

① Heavenly Gates

The northeast face of Carrauntoohil is a confusing jumble
of ribs and it's difficult to make out the line of Howling from
a distance, however the start of route is unambiguous and
once en-route it's just a matter of following the ridge. As
many parties don't pitch the whole climb and the exact route
taken varies, a detailed route description isn't very useful.

Start on the uphill side of the Heavenly Gates. Four steep
sections, which are interspersed with low angle, easier
ground, lead to the steepest most difficult climbing on the
route, The Tower.

From the top of The Tower another steep section leads to
The Finger, a distinctive rock resembling a closed fist with
one finger pointing down the valley that juts out of the right
side of the ridge. It's an obvious landmark and visible on the
skyline from the start of the route.

Above The Finger a tilted horizontal slab known as The
Bridge connects Howling Ridge to Primroses. Two more
steep sections lead to some spectacular but easy climbing
over pinnacles (see photo on page 92) before the final short
steep section leads to the end of the ridge where you can
put away the rope and make the short walk to the summit.
C. Moriarty, J. Cronin February 1987

There are three options for descending from the summit of
Carrauntoohil:

• Heavenly Gates - Follow the path towards the Devil's
Ladder. At approximately GR V 805 838 contour to the
left away from the main path looking for the small track
that leads to the Heavenly Gates. This is probably the best
descent but the start of the path can be hard to find in low
visibility.
• Brother O'Shea's Gully - From the summit of Carrauntoohil
follow a magnetic bearing of 230° for 50m before turning
to 308° and descending the steep zig-zag path to
Cummeenoughter, Ireland's highest lake.
• Devil's Ladder - From Carrauntoohil follow a magnetic
bearing of 192° until you meet the track, then follow this to
the saddle between Carrauntoohil and Cnoc na Toinne. The
Devil's Ladder takes the steep, loose gully down to the valley
floor.

County Kerry
GAP OF DUNLOE
APPROACH **1-30 minutes**
ROCK **Sandstone**
D-S **1** - HS-HVS **23** - E1-E3 **18** - E4+ **2**

The Gap of Dunloe contains over 300 routes spread across more than a dozen crags. The rock is very high quality red sandstone and tends to form steep faces that are crossed by horizontal breaks.

The climbing is generally steep with good holds. The abundance of parallel cracks and breaks make a good selection of cams almost indispensable. Double ropes are useful, especially on the longer pitches, they are also required for the abseil descents.

CONDITIONS

The majority of the routes face east and only get the sun earlier in the day. The valley shelters the crags from the prevailing wind and seepage isn't a much of a problem so the Gap is a good option during the colder, damper months.

DIRECTIONS

From Killarney take the N72 west. After 6km turn left (signposted 'Gap of Dunloe'). After another 4km turn left again (signposted 'Gap of Dunloe') following the road past Kate Kearney's pub.

During the summer months, when the Gap is busy with horse-drawn carts carrying tourists, you should park in Kate's carpark and walk up the road. The rest of the year you can drive, there is room for a few cars on the grass verge just past Brennan's Leap. If this is full then park on the left side of the road just past the bridge.

FACING PAGE Damien O'Sullivan on Out of My Reach HVS 5a, The Main Face (see page 111).

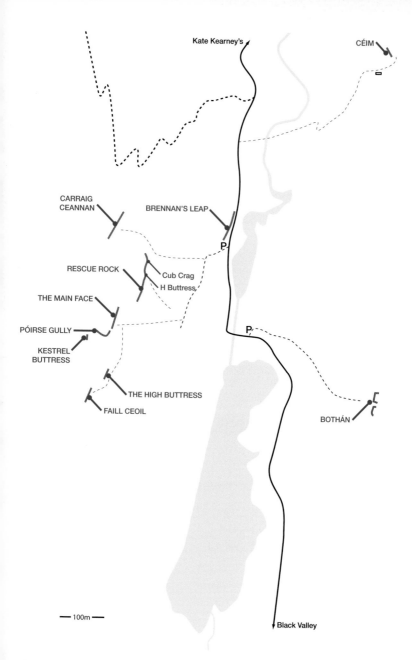

CÉIM

This small crag is a godsend on windy, damp days as it's very sheltered, however avoid it during the summer when it's a haven for the midges. From the road cross the river on stepping stones and follow the grassy track towards the wooded hill. Pass the derelict house and walk down the steep grassy slope, the crag is on your left.

1 **Moondance** VS 4c	15m

Nice climbing up the centre of the crag. A gift at VS compared to Titanic.
D. Tagney, A. Forde 12/10/1994

2 **The Great War** HVS 5a	15m

Climb the slab and finish via the small roof.
R. Stack, G. Stack 11/11/1990

3 **Titanic** VS 4b	12m

The short but steep hand crack. Take!
M Shea, P. Cuff Summer 1985

Cuff's Crap VS 4c
The Black Stuff HVS 5a
Sean Nós HVS 5a
Miss Piggy VS 4c
The Prodigal Son HVS 5a

BOTHÁN

A popular crag with fine views over the valley. It's exposed to the wind so dries quickly and gets the sun later in the day. To get there pass Brennan's Leap and cross the stile just beyond the bridge, following a vague path up to the crag.

4 **Agent Orange** HS 4b
15m

Follow the short left-facing corner to a small ledge then climb the corner just to the right moving right around the overlap just below the top.
I. Counihan, A. Forde 15/09/1990

5 **Private Investigations** VS 4c
20m

Climb directly up to the higher vegetated ledge. Finish up the wall above.
C. Moriarty, M. Shea August 1986

6 **Ljubljana** E1 5c
20m

A great line through the roof, finishing up the blunt arete.
R. Stack, B. Forde 03/08/1991

7 **Disco Legs** E3 5c
20m

A direct line, sustained but well protected.
P. Hoy 04/09/1999

8 **Raven** VS 4b
20m

A great route. An awkward start up the chimney leads to a good ledge on the left. Traverse left across the ledge to the vertical crack and follow this to the top. See photo on facing page.
C. Moriarty, K. Tarrant 1985

FACING PAGE Rory Dalton on Raven VS 4b. Photo by Richard Creagh.

FAILL CEOIL

Faill Ceoil is the furthest crag from the road, it takes about 30 minutes walk to get to it but it's well worth the effort. Follow vague paths from the bridge or Brennan's Leap to the base of The High Buttress and continue south across the slope before scrambling up to the left side of the crag. Descend by abseiling from the bolts above The Sign and Meltdown or very carefully on foot via the heather slopes to the north.

9 **The Sign** E5 6a   60m

An impressive line through the large roof.
P1   25m Poorly protected. Climb directly to the left end of the roof and belay on the large block.
P2   10m Move up from the ledge for a few moves before wildly campusing out along the overlap to belay at the lip of the roof. The in-situ pegs may be less than trustworthy.
P3   25m Climb the wall directly following a crack through the overlaps.
C. Moriarty, M. Shea 05/08/1990
FFA S. Villanueva O'Driscoll, K. Power, E. Kennedy 17/04/2010

10 **Meltdown** HVS (5a,5b)   45m

A stunning route, with a wild first pitch and steep, juggy second pitch. Carry plenty of cams.
P1   23m Climb the corner on the right of the face to a small roof, traverse right to a ledge and continue diagonally right to belay at the small ledge (medium cams).
P2   22m Follow a fairly direct line up the face through a weakness in the overlap to a bolted belay.
A. Forde, A. Devlin April 1986

11 **Kudos** VS (4c,4c)   50m

Brilliant, one of the few lower grade multi-pitch routes in the Gap.
P1   25m Start as for Meltdown. After 3m move right to a ledge. Traverse right across the slab to a crack and corner, climb this to the overlap. Move left and then step right under the square overlap. Move up and left to the Meltdown belay.
P2   25m Climb the wall heading for the base of the corner, passing a small wedged block en route. Follow the corner to the overlap that crosses the face. Move right and then up and left to good holds. Follow a curving ramp on the right to finish just left of the protruding block.
A. Forde, I. Sheahan 13/07/1996

12 **Bosch** E1 5b   25m

The first pitch is a good alternative start to Meltdown. Climb a slightly left-trending crack line before stepping up and right to a corner/crack system which trends slightly right. Follow this to the large ledge and a tree belay.
A. Forde, R. Stack 04/10/1997

Burnt
Ledge

⑬ ⑭ ⑮ ⑯ ⑰

THE HIGH BUTTRESS

As many routes on High Buttress share belays it's possible to mix and match pitches from different climbs. Abseil from the bolts at the top of Scairbhin.

13 **Jamaica Plain** HVS (5a,5a,4b,5a)   70m

P1   30m Follow the corner system moving slightly left and then right and belay on the large ledge below the offwidth crack.
P2   7m Climb the offwidth and move left to the ledge with the holly tree.
P3   20m Climb onto the arete above the offwidth and continue up the left side of the face above to Burnt Ledge.
P4   13m Start on the left edge of the face, climb to the prominent corner, follow a line just right of the crack to the top (crux).
A. Forde, M Shea 1985

14 **Seventh Heaven** E1 (4c,5b)   50m

A good route despite an awkward start.
P1   25m Start at the small tree. Climb the corner over large overhanging blocks and move directly up to belay just above the grassy ledge.
P2   25m Move up to and climb the offwidth (that is shared with Jamaica Plain). Traverse right under the roof to the ledge (protected by small cams). From the far end of the ledge climb directly up to Burnt Ledge.
G. Sexton, C. Moriarty 25/08/1990

15 **The Unforgettable Fire** HVS (4c,5a,5a,4b)   73m

P1   20m Follow the crack through the overlap to a large grassy ledge.
P2   20m Traverse right along the ramp, around the corner and down slightly to a steep, shallow groove that is followed to a belay at the large ledge (large hex).
P3   20m Traverse the ledge above the main roof. Midway along, climb the wall between two parallel cracks to Burnt Ledge, emerging just right of a large boulder.
P4   13m Climb directly up the wall through the weakness in the overhang.
C. Moriarty, M. Shea February 1986

16 **Scairbhin** E1 (5a,5b)   40m

Start 5m right of The Unforgettable Fire beneath a square-cut groove.
P1   20m Climb the groove and exit slightly right over blocks. Continue directly but more easily over large blocks to a belay beneath the next wall (large cam/hex useful).
P2   20m Follow the faint groove to a ledge above a small tree. Continue up left of a dubious flake, through a slight overhang to easier ground and chain belay.
C. Moriarty, M Shea 08/09/1990

17 **Bimbi Limbo** VS (4a,4c)   40m

P1   25m Step up left onto the grassy ledge. Climb up over blocks and ledges just left of the arete. Avoid the overhanging blocks by moving right, climb the short corner and step left to a spacious belay ledge.
P2   15m Climb the arete in a nice exposed position.
A. Forde, R. Stack 18/06/1991

Peregrine Ledge.

PÓIRSE GULLY

The clean buttress at the top left of Póirse Gully is known as Kestrel Buttress and it contains a few worthwhile routes. Descend by abseil or walk around to the top of the gully and scramble down the scree.

18 **Púncánach** E1 5b   20m

Climb the crack/corner system on the left of the buttress. Bolt belay.
A. Forde, I. Counihan March 1990

19 **Bundánach** E2 5c   20m

The direct line up the middle of the face. Gear can be placed left of the line to protect the moves to the first good break. Bolt belay.
S. Hennessey, J. Healy 2007

20 **Kestrel** VS 4c   18m

Climbs the right side of the right arete. Either start from the large boulder or from the bottom of the face. A good selection of cams is required. Bolt belay.
C. Moriarty, D. Mulcahy 1985

The steep wall that forms the north side of the gully has a number of superb routes, especially at E1 and above. Descend via the gully, taking care not to dislodge any loose blocks.

21 **Life In Windy Weather** E1 5b   25m

Climb through the alcove and the overhang above it. Finish up the corner.
A. Forde, N. Gregory 30/04/1990

22 **The Stoop** E2 5c   30m

One of the best routes in the Gap. Climb directly up to the right edge of the block and traverse left to a good rest. Move right in a very exposed position onto the face above the overhang and climb directly to the top. See photo on page 88.
A. Forde, R. Stack 07/05/1995

23 **Air Time** E5 6a   30m

Brilliant climbing, good gear. Climb the steep wall to the right side of the large roof. Arrange gear at the back and campus across the break. Finish up the headwall above.
S. Hennessey, J. O'Raw 2007

24 **Echo Beach** E1 5c   30m

Hard for the grade. Follow a line of good holds diagonally up and right to Peregrine Ledge. Climb the arete from the ledge, moving left around the overhang and finishing over two easy steps.
A. Forde, J. Price 1985

25 **Sun Dogs** E1 (5b,5c)   30m

P1   10m Boldly climb the shallow groove just left of the cave.
P2   20m Start right of Echo Beach and climb the centre of the face through the two overlaps.
R. Stack, A. Forde 05/05/1995

26 **Peregrine** VS 4c   12m

Unusual climbing that requires some old-school chimney technique. Shuffle across the ledge into the cave. Step off the block and climb the wall until forced outwards. Rejoin the vertical and scramble up to Peregrine Ledge.
C. Moriarty I. Counihan 1990

The following routes start from Peregrine Ledge, reach it by climbing one of the previous routes or by scrambling up to the ledge from the back.

27 **Thank You Ivan, Thank You Lord** HVS 5b   15m

Start at the large chockstone wedged between the face and the ledge and take a direct line to the top.
A. Forde, I. Counihan 30/04/1990

28 **Red Dragon** VS 4c   10m

Climb the right edge of the wall.
R. Stack, P. Costelloe 29/09/1991

Come to
the Edge

32

30

31

29

THE MAIN FACE

The tall, clean Main Face has some of the best long pitches in the Gap. Descend by abseiling from the bolts at the top of Out of My Reach or by walking south and scrambling down Póirse Gully. Remember to check for climbers below before throwing your abseil ropes.

29 **P'U** - **Carraigs** E2 (5b,5c)   55m

A link-up of the best pitches of two routes.

P1   30m Start at the foot of the arete and move left and then right rejoining the arete at half height. Step around the arete to a ledge on the right. Move straight up and regain the arete, following it to the top. **Come to the Edge** E2 5b is a bold variation that sticks to the arete.

P2   25m Strenuous. Scramble across the ledge and follow a broken crack through a breach in the overhangs. Bolted belay.
P. Pritchard, A. Forde 07/04/1990

The following routes can, with some careful rope management, be enjoyed in one long pitch.

30 **Out Of My Reach** HVS 5a   45m

A popular route that climbs the left side of the face to the right of the black water stain. The black water stain often seeps but dries quickly. Start from the pedestal at the base of the wall. Move up and then diagonally right along a series of small ledges until you can go directly towards the hanging blocks, pass these on the left and move up to the ledge (optional belay). Poorly protected. Climb the wall behind the tree keeping just right of the black streak. At the top of the black streak move right following a series of sloping ledges to a groove. Climb the groove and head straight up to the bolt belay. See photo on page 96.
C. Moriarty, R. Gabbett 1985

31 **The Overlap** E3 6a   45m

A brilliant pitch. Climb directly to the base of the blank groove, climb this and move left and then up. Swing through the overlap and head directly for the top over easier ground.
A. Forde, C. Moriarty 23/04/1990

32 **Demasiado** E1 5b   40m

A terrific route that makes it way through some steep ground. Climb directly up to the white wall, step right to a small ledge and move left across the sloping ramp. Move up to a small ledge beneath the overlap (optional belay). Breach the overlap on good holds on the left and continue up to a right trending corner. At the top of the corner move diagonally left to the chains.
A. Forde, I. Counihan 01/05/1990

CARRAIG CEANNAN

Good steep climbing. Seepage can be an issue, the rock needs a day or two to dry after heavy rain. Descend from the first two routes by abseiling from the bolts at the top of Cuchulainn.

33 **Cuchulainn** HVS 5a   30m

Tackles the steep crack that runs up the middle of the crag.
C. Moriarty, A. Forde July 1984

34 **Ferdia** HVS 5a   26m

From the start of Cuchulainn climb up and right into a corner, follow this until forced right to a large ledge. Continue up the narrow chimney to the roof, move awkwardly right, and finish up the niche.
A. Forde, C. Moriarty July 1984

35 **Bash on Regardless** E2 5c   25m

Sustained. Follow the shallow groove right of the wide crack (**Moloise** HVS 5b) through the bulge and finish delicately up the face. Belay at the holly tree and abseil off.
A. Forde, A. Devlin November 1985

36 **Black Friday** E2 5b   20m

Start a few metres right of Bash on Regardless. Climb, without much protection to a horizontal quartz vein, traverse right to a horizontal finger crack and move up to a small ledge at mid-height. Continue up and left to a large flake, climb the flake and move up to a large ledge and then move further right to belay at the holly tree. Abseil off.
A. Forde, R. Stack 13/04/1990

RESCUE ROCK

A popular area with some worthwhile shorter routes. Descend via the steep gully between Umbongo and The Crazy Horseman.

37 **Free at Last** HVS 5a
10m

Bold climbing up the middle of the slab. The left side of the slab is **Skyline** S.
M. Shea, R. Stack 09/09/1990

38 **Umbongo** S
10m

The right arete. The wall to the right is tackled by **The Crazy Horseman** E3 6a.
Unknown

39 **Quartz Movement** VS 4c
10m

Climb the right edge of the face. **Rescue Rock** S climbs the left side of the wall.
R. Stack, T. Long 04/05/1995

40 **Mother Of Prague** E1 5b
20m

Climb the middle of the slab to the block. Move up and right into the groove capped by the overlap. From the top of the groove traverse left along a slopey break and finish up the thin crack.
I. Counihan, M. Barry July 1990

41 **Willie Wonka** E2 6a
20m

Climb the right side of the slab to the block and move up to the groove. Make hard moves through the overlap and continue directly to the top.
R. Stack, P. Costelloe 27/12/1989

BRENNAN'S LEAP

A popular, accessible little crag. There are bolts for belaying about 5m back from the top.

42 **Cronin's Crack** HS 4b
10m

The line of least resistance up the centre of the crag.
D. Maguire, P. Cronin 1967

43 **Daffodils** VS 4c
10m

The prominent left-trending crack.
A Forde, C. Moriarty 1984

44 **Rush Hour** HVS 5b
10m

Nice climbing passing the overlap at mid-height.
R. Stack, C. Moriarty 09/07/1990

Granuaile E1 5b
Fat Boys Don't Fall E1 5c
Evening Falls VS 4c
Deadline E3 6a
Movies HVS 4c

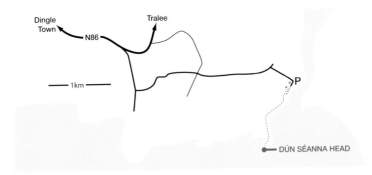

County Kerry
DÚN SÉANNA HEAD
APPROACH **15 minutes**
ROCK **Sandstone**
D-S **1** - HS-HVS **10** - E1-E3 **3** - E4+ **2**

The sandstone sea cliffs of Dún Séanna Head just east of Dingle Town offer some superb single-pitch routes in a very atmospheric setting. The rock is steep with plenty of positive holds. Most of the routes follow cracks or corners but the standout feature is the slender sea stack known as The Needle.

The routes on the west section of the crag can only be accessed by abseil, so an abseil rope is essential. It's possible to scramble down to the platform below the routes on the east side. Most routes are well protected but carry plenty of gear as the pitches are long.

CONDITIONS

The crag faces south and is a good option during the colder months. The climbing isn't affected by the tide but if the sea is rough the start of many routes can be wet. As always when climbing on sea cliffs be alert for rouge waves.

DIRECTIONS

Drive east out of Dingle Town on the N86. After just under 2km turn right (signposted 'Dún Síon'). After 500m turn left, drive to the end of road and park. Access to the crag is via farmer's fields so please respect their property, making sure to close gates after you. Ask permission in advance (066 9151265) and remember camping isn't permitted on the headland or on the beach.

From the carpark walk west along the edge of the fields aiming for the top of the raised headland, the crag is on the far side of this. The routes are described from left to right (as you face the rock).

FACING PAGE David Flanagan on Giraffe VS 4c (see page 119). Photo by Peter McMahon.

Coisceim

Thriller

THE NEEDLE

Set up anchors on the blocks above Giraffe and abseil down Stinky Phoo to the platform where the stack meets the cliff.

1 **The Razor's Edge** VS 4c   30m

An excellent adventure. From the platform traverse right to the sharp, exposed arete which is followed to the top. Beware of loose rock near the summit.
M. Barry, P. Quinn, T. Macken July 1984

2 **Jumbo** E1 5b   25m

A harder route up the steep north wall. From the platform and follow the rightmost of the two cracks to the quartz line, then traverse left and follow a thin crack to the top.
A. Devlin, M. Barry May 1984

Descend the Needle by abseiling down the north face to the platform, bring a long sling for an anchor (don't trust the in-situ tat) then either jumar back up your abseil rope or climb out via J.J. Barry or Stinky Phoo.

THE MAIN FACE

Both of the following routes start from the platform at the base of the Needle.

3 **J.J. Barry** VS 4c   40m

Exposed and sparsely protected. Climb the arete above the left side of the platform, after 30m traverse right along a narrow ledge and finish up Stinky Phoo.
J. Reville, B. Denton, J. Duignan 24/07/2010

4 **Stinky Phoo** HVS 5b   40m

Nice climbing up the prominent corner just right of the Needle. Start by climbing down from the platform to the foot of the corner which is followed to the top. The face on the far side of the right arete is taken by **Thriller** E3 6a.
M. Barry, T. Macken November 1984

The following routes are accessed by scrambling down east of Peter Pan. The platform is non-tidal but it can be swept by waves if the sea is rough so be careful.

5 **Giraffe** VS 4c   40m

Dramatic, well protected climbing up the crack on big holds. Requires a calm sea. See photo on page 116.
M. Barry, T. Macken June 1984

6 **Uncle Alister** HVS 5a   40m

The prominent crack. (The bottom of the route is obscured in the topo). A worthwhile variant **Coiscéim** HVS 5a starts up Giraffe before traversing right to Uncle Alister.
M. Barry, T. Hacken August 1985

The next four routes climb the steep slab.

7 **Heartbeat City** E3 5c

30m

Climb boldy up to a horizontal break, over a bulge and straight up the yellow lichen wall to better holds. Traverse right to the shallow corner and straight up to finish. See photo above.
D. Tangney, T. Macken May 1995

8 **Garden of Earthly Delights** E4 6a/b

30m

Start up Heartbeat City but move diagonally right to the flaky crack. Follow the groove, passing two bolts before moving left into Broad Street.
A. Forde, D. Tangney September 1995

9 **Broad Street** E4 6a

33m

Start just left of a shallow rock pool. Climb up to the flaky crack before moving with difficulty into the groove on the left. Follow this to the top.
E. Cooper, C. Torrans, M. Barry May 1985

10 **Fada Amach** E2 5c

33m

Climb the corner right of the slab.
M. Barry, T. Macken June 1984

ABOVE Dave McBride on Heartbeat City E3 5c. Photo by Richard Creagh.

Hot
Chocolate

⑪ ⑫ ⑬ ⑭ ⑮

Openers

Nutella

16

17

The series of corners between the steep wall and the descent are home to plenty of interesting easier routes.

11 **Grand Larceny** HVS 5a	30m

The rounded arete just right of Fada Amach.
T. Hacken 1985

12 **Deliverance** VS 4c	27m

Follow the shallow groove passing right around the overlap. **Hot Chocolate** E1 5b shares the same start but takes a more direct line to the top.
M. Barry, A. Devlin April 1984

13 **Panache** HS 4b	22m

The corner with a steep finish. See photo on the facing page.
M. Barry, P. Quinn April 1984

14 **Banana Split** VS 4c	27m

The groove just right of Panache.
T. Macken, M.Barry May 1984

15 **Strange Meeting** VS 4c	20m

Well protected, technical climbing in a fantastic position. Start on the left side of the blunt arete between Thievery and Panache. Follow a series of very small ramps and flakes to a horizontal quartz break. From here step around to the right side of the arete and continue straight up to the top. A more direct start up the right side of the blunt arete is possible but there isn't much protection.
E. Cooper, C. Torrans, May 1985

16 **Thievery** HS 4b	22m

The steep, well protected chimney. The two cracks to the right are **Openers** S 4a and **Nutella** HS 4b
A. Devlin, P. Quinn April 1984

17 **Peter Pan** VD	16m

The stepped diagonal ramp.
P. Kelliher, T. Macken April 1984

FACING PAGE Jasmine Eldred on Panache HS 4b. Photo by Richard Creagh.

County Clare

AILLADIE

APPROACH **5 minutes**
ROCK **Limestone**
D-S **0** - HS-HVS **7** - E1-E3 **19** - E4+ **17**

The 800m long limestone sea cliff at Ailladie is considered one of the best crags in the country. The rock is rough and generally sound. The crag is almost entirely vertical and the majority of the routes follow thin cracks or corners.

The best routes are E2 and above. The relatively small number of easier routes aren't quite of comparable quality and tend to be hard for the grade. Most routes are well protected but, as the rock is relatively smooth, cams have a tendency to slip when fallen on so nuts should be used rather than cams where possible. An abseil rope is vital for the routes accessed by abseil.

It's worth bearing in mind that as the cliff takes the full force of the Atlantic, winter storms can remove rock, loosen holds and shift boulders affecting the difficulty of some routes especially the starts.

CONDITIONS

The northern end of the cliff lies above the platform known as the Dancing Ledges, it isn't affected by sea conditions however the routes further south, which lie directly above the sea, may not be climbable when the sea is rough. The routes on Mirror Wall can only be accessed on foot at low tide otherwise you must abseil.

The rock dries very quickly after rain, especially if it's windy but damp may linger in some of the deeper cracks.

DIRECTIONS

From Limerick take the M18 as far as Ennis, then the N85 to Ennistymon and the N67 to Lisdoonvarna. Coming from the north take the N67 south as far as Lisdoonvarna. In Lisdoonvarna take the R477 (signposted 'Coast Road'). After a few miles the sea is visible on the left and the long, low wall of Ballyryan comes into view on the right. Park on the right a little further on.

FACING PAGE Marek Belopotocky on Great Balls of Fire HVS 5a (see page 146). Photo by Juraj Navratil.

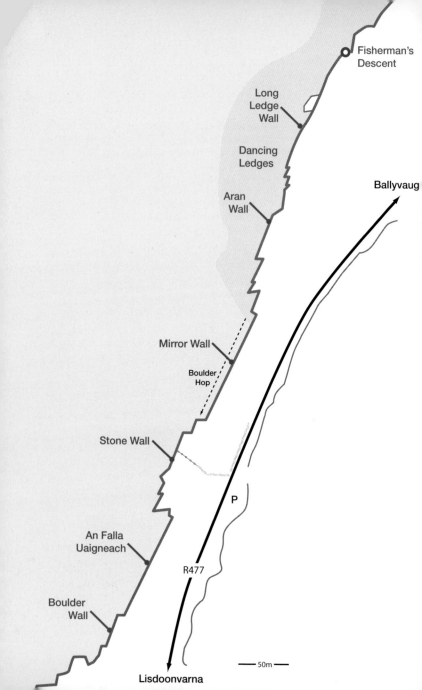

Fisherman's Descent

Long Ledge Wall

Dancing Ledges

Ballyvaug

Aran Wall

Mirror Wall

Boulder Hop

Stone Wall

P

An Falla Uaigneach

R477

Boulder Wall

50m

Lisdoonvarna

LONG LEDGE WALL

From the parking area, pass through the gap in the stone wall, and walk north along the edge of the cliff. After about 500m the cliff becomes significantly lower and it's possible to scramble down a series of ledges known as the Fisherman's Descent to the Dancing Ledges. The following routes are extremely popular, a fact that is reflected in the polished holds.

1 **Ground Control** VS 4c   16m

Steep, well protected climbing. Start below the left-trending cracks and make a hard move to the ledge (trivial for the tall) and climb the diagonal crack above.
T. Ryan, D. Windrim, K. Higgs August 1976

2 **Genesis** HS 4b   16m

The steep groove is popular and awkward in equal measure.
J. Mulhall, S. Young 07/08/1972

3 **Bonnan Bui** VS 4c   15m

Steep and hard for the grade. Start just left of the arete and climb broken ground to the groove which is followed to the top. The crux is getting established in the groove.
J. Mulhall, J. McKenzie 26/11/1972

4 **Nutrocker** HVS 5a   15m

Strenuous laybacking up the steep corner just right of Bonnan Bui, easier for the tall.
S. Young, J. Mulhall 07/08/1972
FFA J. Levy May 1975

ARAN WALL

The long, vertical wall is packed with routes of the highest quality.

5 **Gallows Pole** E2 5c
28m

This classic route climbs the pair of parallel cracks that start halfway up the wall.
K. Higgs, T. Ryan, S. Windrim 21/08/1977

6 **Marchanded Crack** E2 5b
28m

After a bold start the climbing eases.
B. Richardson, J. Levy May 1975

7 **Midnight Summer Dream** E3 5c   28m

Step right from Marchanded Crack at mid-height and climb the crack.
T. Ryan, K. Murphy 18/09/1982

8 **Desolation Row** E4 6a   28m

A variant of a variant but interesting nonetheless. See photo on page 134.
E. Cooper, C. Torrans April 1984

9 **Sunstone** E3 6a   30m

Difficult climbing gains the steep, sustained crack.
T. Ryan, D. O'Connell 25/05/1983

10 **Eliminator** E5 6b   28m

Traverse left under the overhang and move up to the crack. Follow this, the crux
comes at the overlap.
D. O'Sullivan 12/08/1985

11 **Kleptomaniac** E3 6a   29m

Magnificent climbing, sustained and strenuous. See photo on the facing page.
K. Murphy, T. Ryan August 1982

12 **Grey Dawn** E5 6b   30m

Follow Point Blank to the ledge and climb the thin crack on the left.
H. Hebblethwaite August 1988

13 **Point Blank** E5 6b   30m

Superb technical climbing.
E. Cooper, C. Torrans 04/06/1985
FFA G. Gibson 1986

14 **Lucy** E2 5c   32m

Steep climbing up the wide crack. The crux is the headwall at the top.
K. Murphy, T. Ryan 18/09/1982

15 **Stigmata** E6 6b   32m

A thrilling route that climbs the central groove.
C. Waddy 1986

16 **Skywalker** E2 5c   32m

A popular route up the crack that skirts the right hand side of the huge projecting
block.
K. Murphy, T. Ryan September 1981

FACING PAGE Richard Creagh on Kleptomaniac E3 6a. Photo by Pat Nolan.

17 **Stardust** E3 5c   25m

Strenuous climbing up the steep corner. Finish up the thin crack.
T. Ryan, K. Murphy May 1984

18 **Very Big Springs** E7 6b   25m

The desperate thin crack.
G. Smith 1993

19 **Ice Queen** E5 6a   25m

A bold route that weaves up the middle of the wall. A bold, fingery start gains better
protection. Finish up the thin crack.
G. Gibson, M. Manson, J. Codling 24/06/1985

20 **Wall Of Fossils** E4 6a   25m

A classic. Climb the groove and overlap. Follow an easier groove to the overhang
and step left on good holds. Finish up the thin crack (crux).
K. Murphy, T. Ryan 22/07/1984

21 **Fall Of Wossils** E5 6a   25m

An impressive and unusual pitch. Follow Wall of Fossils to the headwall and move
right with difficulty to the arete which is climbed on its right side.
G. Gibson, M. Manson, J. Codling 23/06/1985

FACING PAGE Peter Linney on Desolation Row E4 6a (see page 133). Photo by Dave Ayton.

MIRROR WALL

The stunning, plumb vertical wall south of The Dancing Ledges is home to some of the best routes in the country. The starts of the next four routes are reached by abseil.

Peanut
Butter Special

22 **Refraction** E5 6a
28m

Outstanding. Abseil to the ledge and belay below the crack. Follow the thin finger
crack to a rest where it crosses the diagonal overlap. Continue more easily until the
cracks narrows, hard moves and a peg lead to the top.
J. Codling, G. Gibson, M. Manson 23/06/1985

23 **Virtual Image** E3 6a
26m

Brilliant climbing in a superb situation. Abseil to the small ledge. Climb the thin crack, with the crux coming early before a rest at the horizontal break.
K Murphy, T. Ryan 19/09/1982

24 **Zebedee** E4 6a
27m

A more strenuous alternative to Virtual Image. Follow Virtual Image to mid-height where a crack branches up and right. The crux is the thin crack just below the top.
D. O'Sullivan, C. O'Cofaigh July 1991

25 **The Cutter** E4 6a
30m

Abseil to a ledge at the base of the crack. Follow the superb sustained crack to the top.
G. Gibson, J. Codling 24/6/1985

The following routes can be accessed at low tide by crossing the boulders at the foot of Mirror Wall otherwise you must abseil.

26 **Through The Looking Glass** E3 5c
36m

An excellent climb. Belay on left end of the narrow ledge. Follow the groove to a sloping ledge. Climb the thin crack (crux) to a horizontal break and continue up the crack which widens near the top.
K. Murphy, T. Ryan August 1982

27 **On Reflection** E6 6a
30m

A magnificent route, sustained with only adequate protection. Climb the groove and move boldly right to a shelf. Continue straight up the cracks to the top.
G. Gibson, M. Manson, J. Codling 23/06/1985

28 **The Ramp** E1 (5b,5a)
45m

A superb line and the easiest route on Mirror Wall. See photo on facing page.
P1 28m Start from the ledge and make hard moves up the corner before following the ramp to a belay on the ledge.
P2 17m Follow the ledges right to a short corner. Climb the corner and finish up the wall above.
D. Somers, J. Dwyer 09/07/1977
FFA C. Torrans 1977

29 **Quicksilver** E5 6a
31m

A brilliant route. Climb the first few metres of the corner until it's possible to traverse left to the base of a thin crack. Follow this until it peters out, make hard moves up to better holds and continue up the sustained wall above, finishing up the thin crack.
E. Cooper, S. McEvoy June 1988

FACING PAGE Shauna Clarke on The Ramp E1 (5b,5a). Photo by Daniel Moore.

Peanut
Butter
Sepcial

31

30 32 33 34

The southern end of Mirror Wall has a series of cracks and chimneys, taken by **Peanut Butter Special** VS (4b,4b) and while not of the highest quality it's a handy escape route.

30 **Black Baron** E2 5b   30m

Excellent climbing with spaced protection. Start on the boulders below the arete left of Pis Fliuch. Climb the crack just right of the arete. Place gear near the top of the crack and then climb down until it's possible to traverse left on small holds to a sloping ledge. Move right around the overlap, climb the groove to an overhang, pass under this on the right and finish up a groove with one last hard move.
T. Ryan, K. Murphy 19/09/1982

The steep smooth wall left of the prominent corner of Pis Fluich is home to a trio of sustained, well protected crack climbs of the highest quality.

31 **Joker Man** E6 6b   30m

Follow Black Baron to the top of the groove and continue directly up the thin crack above, briefly moving left to the arete near the top.
E. Cooper 20/05/1988
FFA E. Cooper 04/05/1996

32 **Damn The Torpedoes** E6 6b   30m

Follow the left-hand crack to the horizontal break, make hard moves left to the crack which is followed to the top.
E. Cooper 1992

33 **Sharkbait** E5 6b   30m

Climb the right-hand of the two cracks.
H. Hebblethwaite June 1988
FFA E. Cooper 1992

34 **Pis Fluich** HVS 5a   30m

The perfectly formed corner is an intimidating classic. See photo on the facing page.
J. McKenzie, J. Mulhall 25/11/1972

35 **Key Largo** E3 5c   30m

A dramatic and serious route. Abseil to the small ledge near the base of the arete or belay on the boulders below. Follow the steep ramp (crux) to a ledge. Either climb the arete directly to the top or move left and over the overlap before gaining the arete.
C. Torrans, D. O'Sullivan 30/09/1984

FACING PAGE Michael Reardon on Pis Fluich HVS 5a. Photo by Damon Corso.

STONE WALL

Stone Wall is easily identified by the fence at the top. Its routes can only be accessed by abseil and while non-tidal they may be unclimbable if the sea is rough.

36 **Garbh** E2 5b
17m

Sustained, thoughtful climbing. Start 7m south of the arete of Key Largo. Abseil to the base of the left-facing corner. Climb the corner and the crack above with a difficult start and an awkward finish.
C. Torrans, C. Sheridan 21/05/1978

37 **Western Pride** E2 5b
12m

Well protected climbing, low in the grade. Abseil to the ledge from a point 3m south of the fence and climb the crack.
C. Parkin, P. Blackburn 19/04/1979

38 **Jug City** VS 4c
12m

Abseil down the corner 15m south of the fence and belay on the southern end of the ledge. Climb the corner making a powerful move halfway up.
T. Ryan, S. Gallwey July 1979

39 **The Emigrant** E2 5c
30m

A full body workout. Abseil down to a large tidal ledge below the corner. Climb the, often damp, overhanging groove to the ledge. Finish up the corner at the back of the ledge.
J. Colton 21/08/1977

40 **Siren** E3 5c
20m

Expect an audience. Superb, committing climbing. Abseil to the ledge just left of the corner and belay. Follow the ramp on the left to a small ledge. Arrange gear in the break just above the ledge and quest up the wall above.
K. Murphy, T. Ryan 18/03/1984

AN FALLA UAIGHNEACH

An Falla Uaigneach, the lonely wall, is also home to some quality deep water soloing on its southern end.

41 **Sea Bird** E1 5b
25m

Spectacular climbing up the middle of the wall. Abseil to a small stance under the prominent overhang (the first section is usually a little damp). Belay on small nuts and the abseil rope. Step right and climb the delicate wall to an overhang. Move left around this and up the corner (crux) to the large overhang. Traverse up and right and finish more easily. See photo on facing page.
M. Smith, M. Manson, T. Ryan 22/05/1981

FACING PAGE Marek Przybylski on Sea Bird E1 5b. Photo by Marek Przybylski.

BOULDER WALL

The top of this steep slab can be identified by the small boulder that lies close to the edge. Directly below the boulder at the foot of the slab is a ledge.

42 **Doolin Rouge** E1 5a
26m

Bold slab climbing. Abseil to the left end of the ledge and belay on the abseil rope. Start up the slab before traversing left to the arete. Follow the arete over a bulge to a reasonable stance. Move up and right to finish.
P. Blackburn, G. Jewson 16/04/1979

43 **Great Balls Of Fire** HVS 5a
26m

A splendid route with a bit of everything. Carry plenty of large gear. Belay on the right end of the ledge. Follow the wide crack to an overlap. Traverse delicately left and finish more easily up the crack. See photo on page 126.
B. Walker, M. Boushell June 1977

The Boulder ⟶

42

43

County Galway

BEN CORR

APPROACH **75 minutes**
ROCK **Quartzite**
D-S **1** - HS-HVS **0** - E1-E3 **0** - E4+ **0**

Carrot Ridge vies with Howling Ridge in Kerry (see page 95) for the title of best
mountain route in Ireland. The ridge runs up the left hand side of a huge quartzite
wall on the south face of Ben Corr in the Twelve Bens, Connemara. It's a popular
route and much like Howling could be considered either an easy climb or a hard
scramble. The rock is clean and for the most part sound with abundant holds. The
stepped ridge stands proud of the surrounding rock and the line is obvious if a little
escapable in places.

The Main Face to the right has two dozen routes but the only one that receives any
attention is the 330m VS **Seventh Heaven** which has something of a reputation for
tricky route finding, scant protection and committing climbing. If that gets your juices
flowing consult www.climbing.ie for more information.

CONDITIONS

Unfortunately the mountains of Connemara are frequently shrouded in cloud when
the coast is bathed in sunshine, but the cloud and rain can disappear as quickly
as it arrived and Carrot Ridge dries quickly as there is minimal vegetation and no
seepage. On still, warm days midges can be a nuisance on the walk-in but are
unlikely to be a problem once you start climbing. The floor of Gleninagh is profoundly
boggy, hiking boots or even wellies are essential if you want dry feet.

DIRECTIONS

From Galway City drive west on the N59. After 55km, shortly after passing through
Recess, turn right onto the R334 (signposted 'Letterfrack'). Pass Lough Inagh on the
left. About 1km after crossing a small bridge turn left onto a narrow road (signposted
'Glen Inagh House B+B') and park considerately at the first house on the right hand
side. Walk to the end of the road. The land you pass through is a working farm
owned by the Bodkins family, you should call into the last house on the right to ask
for permission to pass through.

Follow the track up the valley. Sooner or later leave the track, cross the river and
head directly across some very boggy ground to the distinctive ridge on the left hand
side of the crag. Slog up the scree slope to the foot of the route.

FACING PAGE Dave McCarthy on the Second Step. Photo by Richard Creagh.

DESCENT

Third Step

Second Step

First Step

①

1 **Carrot Ridge** VD   360m

The first pitch is the crux of the route, with delicate climbing on small holds and minimal protection. And while the climbing on the first pitch is enjoyable it could prove quite challenging in the wet while wearing big boots. Avoiding it by traversing into the start of the second pitch from the left brings the grade down to D.

Everyone seems to climb the route slightly differently so the following description is only a rough guide.

P1   50m A bold lead. Start at the foot of the pale pink slab. Climb the slab near its left edge to a stance just below the final steep section (optional belay). Tricky moves lead through the steepness, belay just above. To reach the first belay with a 50m rope the belayer needs to stand a bit higher than the foot of the slab.
P2   30m Move up and then left heading for the large ledge below the vertical wall. Belay at a large boulder. A more challenging option is to move left immediately and then head directly up to the ledge.
P3   45m **The First Step** A steep start off the ledge on big holds leads to a slab, climb this either directly or move right then left to the foot of the corner/chimney (optional belay). Climb the chimney and belay at the top.
P4   90m Scramble along easy, level ground to the foot of the Second Step.
P5   45m **The Second Step** Tackle the short steep wall on its left and then move right to the foot of the groove that runs up the ridge just right of centre. Climb this on lovely big holds to easy ground (see photo on page 148).
P6   100m **The Third Step** Easy scrambling leads to the top of the ridge.
Alberry, Crofton 1933

Descent down the steep scree slope east of the ridge. Alternatively you could continue to the summit of Ben Corr before descending via the Maumina Pass and following the good path back down Gleninagh.

DONEGAL

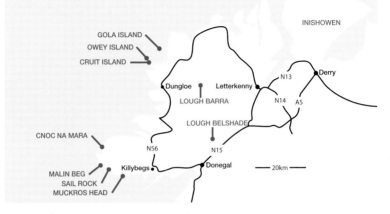

Donegal is a vast county, it takes over three hours to drive from the northern tip to the southwest corner and there is a huge amount of climbing, nearly 3000 routes, in a range of settings and on over a half dozen rock types.

In the southwest there is accessible single-pitch routes at Malin Beg and Muckros Head and more serious adventure climbing on Sail Rock and Cnoc na Mara.

Further up the coast the islands of Gola, Owey and Cruit offer excellent sea cliff climbing in an idyllic setting.

Inland the granite mountain crags of Lough Belshade and Lough Barra have some superb multi-pitch routes.

In the northwest Inishowen has a large selection of crags with plenty of routes in the mid to low grades.

ACCOMMODATION

Rural Donegal is ideal for wild camping and there is no end of scenic, quiet places to stay on the coast and in the hills. Most reasonably sized towns will have a hostel and there are B+Bs everywhere.

OTHER CLIMBING

The Poisoned Glen in the Derryveagh Mountains is home to some of the most impressive cliffs in the country. The huge granite buttresses, up to 200m tall, are rarely visited by contemporary climbers in spite of their obvious potential.

REST/RAINY DAYS

Like the rest of the west coast Donegal is geared towards tourism and there is plenty to see and do when you aren't climbing, see www.govisitdonegal.com for some ideas.

FACING PAGE Andy Marshall on P2 of Main Mast E2 (5b,5c), Sail Rock (see page 163). Photo by Craig Hiller.

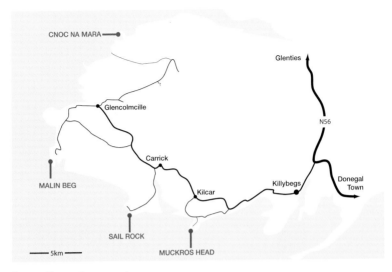

County Donegal

MUCKROS HEAD
APPROACH **2 minutes**
ROCK **Sandstone**
D-S **1** - HS-HVS **6** - E1-E3 **7** - E4+ **4**

Muckros Head is probably the steepest crag in Ireland. The rough sandstone walls are riddled with roofs and positive horizontal breaks, making for strenuous but well protected climbing. Large cams are particularly useful for the plentiful horizontal breaks. The rock is generally very solid but the top of the crag can be a little loose.

CONDITIONS

It's possible to climb at any tide if the sea is calm but on rough days the waves can sweep across the flat platform beneath the crag. Seepage can be an issue but is very difficult to predict.

DIRECTIONS

From Donegal Town drive west on the N56. After 25km turn left onto the R263/ Killybegs Road. About 7km past Killybegs fork left (signposted 'Coast Road'). After another 3km turn left onto a small road (there is a signpost pointing back the way you have just come saying 'Killybegs 10km'). Follow the road and park at the end of the rough track. Walk along the path down to the platform and continue along the base of the crag to the prominent roof of Stormy Petrel.

FACING PAGE Sean Villanueva O'Driscoll on Sideswipe E7 6c (see page 161). Photo by Ben Ditto.

1 **Bombay Duck** S 4a — 15m

The prominent corner on the wall left of the roof.
K. Higgs, C. Torrans 09/04/1977

2 **Tandoori Chicken** E3 5c — 15m

The top of the wall right of Bombay Duck features a prominent flake. Climb easily to the overlap below it and make a tricky move to the flake, layback it and finish easily.
E. Cooper September 1990

3 **Stormy Petrel** E4 6a — 17m

A sensational route crossing the huge roof. Climb easily to the crack that splits the roof. Quest out across the roof to the jugs on the lip.
R. Fenlon, D. O'Sullivan June 1991

4 **Tricky Dicky** VS 4c — 17m

Start (with difficulty) just left of the arete. Move right and up the wall above. **Micky Mouse** E1 5c shares the same start but takes the wall further right to a steep finish.
C. Torrans, K. Higgs 09/04/1977

5 **Cois Farraige** VS 4c — 18m

Another hard start. Once established follow the offset crack up the steep wall.
D. Somers, J. Colton 09/04/1977

6 **Elvis** E3 6a — 17m

The Muckros classic. Use the good pocket to reach the break beneath the roof. Yard across the roof using the trio of pockets. Turn the lip and keep it together up the steep wall above. See photo on facing page.
N. Grimes, A. Millar April 1991

FACING PAGE Marek Przybylski on Elvis E3 6a. Photo by Marek Przybylski.

7 **Morning Glory** HS 4b

17m

Fairly improbably ground for the grade. Start up the steep corner before stepping left to another corner. Climb this, moving left at the top. The sharp arete to the left is the committing **The Cabbage** E2 6a.

J. Colton, D. Somers 09/04/1977

8 **The Barb** E1 5b

18m

Bridge up the corner before moving across and up the steep left wall to a stance on the arete. Swing right and over the roof (crux). Finish up the wall of orange rock above.

S. Windrim, K. Higgs 30/04/1978

9 **Wonderful Stories Jesus Told** E3 6a

18m

An outstanding route, with tons of character, it climbs through the four overhangs that form a series of left-facing corners. The second roof is the crux, after which the difficulty eases somewhat.

B. Callan, N. Grimes June 1991

10 **Granny by Gaslight** E3 5c   18m

Pure thuggery. Climb the corner and reach out for the break. Campus right along the break and around the arete to the base of the wide crack. Climb the crack and finish up the wall above.
A. Millar, N. Grimes May 1991

11 **Never Never Land** E6 6b   20m

A stupendous line. Start in the short corner 20m right of Granny by Gaslight. Climb the corner using the flake on the left. Move right and up to an undercut beneath the first roof. Make a long reach and swing out to traverse right to the next big groove. An awkward rest can be had at the groove by sitting on the ledge. Using the jammed block, pull up and traverse left on small holds to the triangular point of the roof. Finish up the steep wall above (crux).
P. Dunlop May 1993

12 **Headland** VS 4c   30m

Bags of exposure. Follow the left arete of the cave to the horizontal break. Traverse
left across the headwall and finish up the crack just right of the corner. **Boho Dance**
S 4a climbs the wall just to the right.
D. O'Sullivan, R. Fenlon June 1991

13 **Joy of Frogs** HVS 4c   20m

Climb the crack on the left-hand side of the huge block and traverse left along the
horizontal break to the arete. Follow the arete in a superb position to a large ledge.
Finish up the wall above.
D. O'Sullivan, J. Dugdale May 1991

14 **Primula** HVS 5a   18m

Intimidating climbing, weaving around the overhangs. Climb to the top of the huge
block. Start up the corner above, move right beneath the overlap (crux) and then
move back left to the next corner. Finish up this.
C. Torrans, C. Sheridan 09/04/1977

15 **Pump up the Valium** E3 6a   18m

Breath-taking and pumpy. Climb up past a pair of wide breaks, move slightly right
and beef up the steep wall (crux). Take a rest on the ledge on the left before stepping
right and finishing up the groove.
D. O'Sullivan, J. Dugdale May 1991

Sideswipe

16 **Operation Mindcrime** E6 6b   20m

Start as for Flesh and continue directly up the groove in the centre of the wall (#1 and
#1.5 cams in the horizontal break at the top of the groove). Step left and up before
a long move back right gains big holds in a short break (#2.5 cam). One more move
right leads to good jugs before the big sequence on small holds up the very steep
wall above.
P. Dunlop 13/06/1993

17 **Flesh** E5 6a   18m

Stupendous, powerful and outrageous. Start below and 1m left of the thin crack.
Move up to a deep vertical slot and make a hard move up and left to a juggy break.
Move back right to the base of the thin crack and follow it, on improving holds, to the
top.
N. Grimes, B. Callan June 1991

18 **The Importance of Being Elvis** E2 5b   20m

Wandering and intricate, watch out for rope drag. Climb the small corner and head
diagonally left up the overhanging wall to a ledge. Boldy traverse left across the wall
and around the arete into the left-facing corner (crux). Continue over the overlap and
up the gully to finish.
I. McNicholl, B. Catlan June 1991

The cave to the right is home to one of Donegal's hardest routes **Sideswipe** E7 6c,
see photo on page 154.

County Donegal
SAIL ROCK
APPROACH **20 minutes**
ROCK **Quartzite**
D-S **0** - HS-HVS **1** - E1-E3 **1** - E4+ **0**

Among the spectacular choss of Slieve League (Ireland's highest 'cliffs') lies a sweeping slab of quartzite, host to two magnificent routes in a remote and very atmospheric setting.

CONDITIONS

When the sea is calm it's possible to climb at any tide but when it's rough the base of the slab is swept by waves.

DIRECTIONS

From Donegal Town take the N56 west (see map on page 155). After 25km turn left onto the R263. Shortly after crossing the bridge in Carrick turn left (signposted 'Teelin Pier'). Follow the road into the small village of Teelin and turn right (signposted 'Bunglas – Slieve League viewing point'). Pass the first carpark and drive steeply up the hill. After 800m park on the left where the road curves 90° to the right.

Walk along the path towards the signal tower. After 250m descend into the grassy valley on the left, the top of the crag soon comes into view. The best approach is to abseil directly down the line of your chosen route but this requires a 100m rope. The other option is a very exposed scramble down the loose ridge east of the crag.

1 **Roaring Forties** VS (4c,4b,4c)	81m

Superb climbing up the left edge of the slab. The final pitch is outstanding with steep, well protected climbing.
P1   28m Start at the lowest point of the basin and follow the arete to a belay on the grassy ledge level with the basalt dyke.
P2   18m Follow a series of grooves to another platform.
P3   35m Climb up for 10m to a stance and continue up a crack to the top or (even better) break out right onto the face.
D. Scott, R. Gillies May 1967

2 **Main Mast** E2 (5b,5c)	69m

The thin diagonal crack is considered one of the best climbs in the country. See photo on page 152.
P1   33m Climb the broken cracks and slabs to the basalt dyke, easy but bold and can be damp. From the dyke follow the crack to a hanging belay at the small ledge.
P2   36m Very sustained climbing up the crack, which gets thinner and steeper with height, leads to the top.
D. Scott, R. Shaw, D. Nicol August 1967
FFA Ryan, Manson, Prendergast 1981

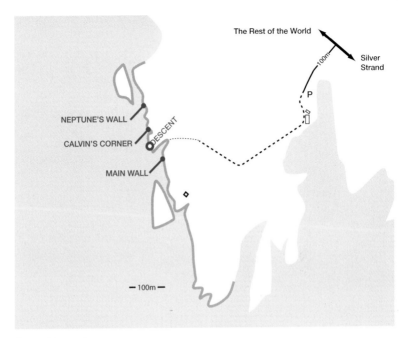

The Rest of the World

Silver
Strand

P

NEPTUNE'S WALL

DESCENT

CALVIN'S CORNER

MAIN WALL

— 100m —

County Donegal
MALIN BEG
APPROACH **5 minutes**
ROCK **Quartzite**
D-S **1** - HS-HVS **6** - E1-E3 **0** - E4+ **0**

The sea cliffs at Malinbeg offer a decent selection of nice routes mostly in the lower grades that are close to the road and on good, clean rock.

CONDITIONS

The climbing isn't tidal, but you may have to approach some routes by abseil at high tide. The crag's exposed position takes the brunt of the prevailing wind and the sea which means that the routes can often be unclimbable due to rough seas.

DIRECTIONS

From Donegal Town take the N56 west (see map on page 155). After 25km turn left onto the R263. 5km past the village of Carrick turn left onto the L1025 (signposted 'Málainn Bhig'). After 10km you reach a junction, turn left and follow the road. Shortly after you pass the Malinbeg Hostel turn right, at the bottom of a hill is small harbour, park here and follow the track on foot to the top of the cliffs.

FACING PAGE Gareth Brown on Fiddler's Green HVS 5a (see page 167). Photo by Richard Creagh..

NEPTUNE'S WALL

The steep pocketed slab known as Neptune's Wall is 100m north of the point where the path meets the coast. Access the base by scrambling down from the north at low tide or else abseil in. The routes are short and well protected with positive holds.

1 **Shaky Rigging** HS 4b   15m

Follow a crack on the left edge of the wall to a ledge, step right onto the face and climb to the top on small holds.
D. Byrne, P. O'Connor 13/04/1979

2 **The Bosun's Ladder** S 4a   15m

Climb the vertical crack 2m right of Shaky Rigging.
P. Sloane, P. O'Connor, J. Leonard 01/08/1977

3 **Hydrophobia** VS 4b   15m

The centre of the wall. **Carrig Una** D climbs the right end of the wall.
D. Keena, S. Long 09/04/1978

CALVIN'S CORNER

4 **Calvin's Corner** HS 4b   8m

Just north of the Main Wall is an easy angled slab that is the descent route for the Main Wall. Climb the dark corner that lies north of the slabs.
C. Torrans, S. Billane 24/05/1975

THE MAIN WALL

Access by scrambling down the slabs to the north or, at high tide, abseil.

5 **Lord of the Flies** HS 4b   25m

The lower of the two ramps leads, with one awkward mantleshelf to the foot of a black chimney. Layback the crack (crux) just right of the chimney, and finish up steep ground.
D. Walsh, P. Gargan, C. Wray 20/05/1978

6 **Flying Enterprise** VS 5a   27m

Classic and hard for the grade, the gear is a little spare at times. Make technical moves up the shallow groove to a ledge. A hard move up the blank slab (crux) leads to the upper ramp which is followed to the top.
T. Ryan, J. McKenzie, J. Scott 31/03/1975

7 **Fiddler's Green** HVS 5a   27m

Another must do. Hard moves up the groove lead to the wide ramp. Follow the ramp to the base of the steep corner. Climb this (crux) and continue up the ramp to the top. See photo on page 164.
D. Walsh, D. Webster 20/05/1978

FACING PAGE Climbers on The Bosun's Ladder S 4a and Hydrophobia VS 4b. Photo by Stephen Carson.

OPTIONAL
BELAY

County Donegal

CNOC NA MARA

APPROACH **180 minutes**
ROCK **Choss**
D-S **0** - HS-HVS **1** - E1-E3 **0** - E4+ **0**

Cnoc na Mara, the Hill of the Sea, is one of the best adventure climbs in Ireland.
To reach its summit one hundred metres above the Atlantic is a multi-discipline
undertaking requiring hiking, paddling, ropework and careful climbing on loose rock.

You will need some sort of inflatable boat, paddles, buoyancy aids, helmets and
three ropes (one to leave in place on the descent to the beach and two - ideally
60m - to climb with). The ideal vessel is a cheap two person dingy, light and relatively
sea worthy. Needless to say sea stacking can be extremely dangerous and is only
suitable for experienced climbers.

CONDITIONS

The long days of mid-summer are the perfect time to attempt Cnoc na Mara. A calm
sea is essential to land safely on the stack. And while a little rain won't affect the
climbing too much the grassy slope that leads to the beach would be treacherous
when wet.

DIRECTIONS

From Donegal Town take the N56 west (see map on page 155) for 25km where you
turn right onto the R263, continue straight on through Killybegs, and after 25km you
reach Glencolmcille. Follow the road straight through the village (signposted 'Ardara')
and after 2km turn left (signposted 'Port'). After 7km you come to a junction, turn left
and descend the narrow road to the sea. Park at the end of the road by the beach.
Welcome to the middle of nowhere. See map on page 155.

Walk up the steep grassy slope to the north and follow the path along the cliff top for
2km until you reach the narrow headland overlooking three huge stacks (GR G 557
906). Carefully descend the very steep 250m high grass slope (keep to the grass on
the left and avoid the scree to the right) and abseil down to the pebble beach from
the in-situ pegs at the foot of the band of rock about 40m above the beach. Finally
paddle across the 150m wide channel to the foot of the stack passing the smaller
stack, Lurking Fear, on the right.

FACING PAGE Looking up P4 to the summit. Photo by Iain Miller.

SEA STACKING

Iain Miller, the first ascentist of Cnoc na Mara and over 40 other stacks in Donegal, is the sea stack guru. Iain works as a guide so if you aren't happy climbing one under your own steam get in touch with him, www.uniqueascent.ie. Here Iain offers a little insight into the techniques and equipment required to climb a stack.

And so, having discovered that the rabbit hole does indeed exist in Western Donegal, it was time to discover how deep it really goes and so a journey of solo adventures commenced. The commitment required and the sense of primal fear that accompanies these journeys has to be experienced to be believed.

As always, a tad of logistics and planning is the key to success and of course the adoption of perhaps less orthodox climbing equipment such as 600m of 6mm polyprop, a lightweight Lidl dinghy, a single lightweight paddle, divers booties, a 20ft cordelette, a pair of Speedo's, heavy duty dry bags, 20m of 12mm polyprop, an alpine hammer, a snow bar, a selection of pegs, a chest harness/inverted Gri-Gri combo and a big grin! Some of the more memorable moments have been paddling with dolphins, bull selkies and a massive basking shark, all within 15 foot of my tiny Lidl dinghy up to a kilometre from land.

Alas a moment of mild concern was had whilst taking a 60-foot screamer, landing in the sea and realising there was an angel standing at the base of the stack. Standing on micro summits many, many kilometres from anywhere deep in the knowledge that you are truly alone is the true embodiment of being the owner of dynamic rope! I have refrained from writing anything regarding the safety aspect of adventure climbing suffice to say it is a very dangerous activity and every time I go out to play, the rope work, boat work and planning that accompany these activities is extremely thorough and anal so as to ensure a maximum margin of safety.

I have developed a unique method of nautical access using non-climbing equipment and techniques which would take many pages to describe and explain, so after nearly 100 top-end adventurous days out without serious incident either I am extremely skilled, very lucky or have sold my soul to Neptune; the jury is still out.

But the tale continues ...

THIS PAGE Once more into the deep. Photo by Iain Webster.

Cnoc na Mara

Lurking
Fear

1

Tormore Island

1 **Cnoc na Mara** VS (3c,-,4b,4a)   150m

This route up the 100m high landward arete of the stack was the original route to the summit. The rock is very loose in places, the gear can be unreliable, and the exposure and sense of commitment are off the scale. So don't be fooled by the grade, getting to the top of this stack is hard and the actual climbing is probably the easiest part of the day. And it's a long day with 12 to 14 hours the average time for an ascent car to car.

P1   35m From the ledge climb a blocky groove on nice, solid black rock. Move up onto vegetated ground and follow the groove right of the rib to the ridge. Move around a small tower to belay at the in-situ rope.

P2   20m Scramble easily up the slab to the base of the huge knife edge arete. Belay on one of the boulders just before the series of ledges that lead to the arete.

P3   35m Move up over the ledges to arrive at the arete at the point where a sharp fin protrudes to the right. Make sensational moves to get established on the other side of the arete and follow it to a ledge, peg and block belay.

P4   60m An airy traverse along the sharp ridge leads to the summit. The climbing is mostly very easy, just walking in places, but the exposure is significant. Place plenty of gear to protect both leader and second. The second should unclip the gear but leave it in place for the descent. If you are climbing with 50m ropes you will need to break this pitch into two by belaying after 25m at the foot of the steep section (see photo on page 168).

I. Miller, A. Tees, M. McGuigan 26/07/2008

The descent from the summit is convoluted and time consuming. Pitch 4 is down climbed with the second going first, clipping the gear left behind as they go. The leader then leads down removing the gear. A double rope abseil from anchors on the top of pitch 3 will bring you to the belay at the top pitch 2. From there climb down to the thread belay at the top of pitch 1 where another double rope ab - watch out for bird life - will bring you back to the boat.

LOUGH BELSHADE

APPROACH **120 minutes**
ROCK **Granite**
D-S **0** - HS-HVS **4** - E1-E3 **2** - E4+ **0**

This remote crag lies deep in the Bluestack Mountains above the shore of Lough Belshade. Those who brave the long walk in and are lucky with the weather will be rewarded with some of the best mountain routes in the country on immaculate pink-hued granite. Carry plenty of cams for the parallel cracks that most of the routes follow.

CONDITIONS

The rock seeps for a few days after wet weather. The crag is sheltered by the surrounding slopes so the midges can be horrific during the summer months.

DIRECTIONS

At the time of writing there is an access issue with the traditional approach from the Lough Eske. The next best approach is from the north, unfortunately it's long and complicated, and can't be easily described here. Consult www.rockClimbingInIreland.com for full details and the latest on the access situation.

THIS SPREAD Geoff Thomas on P2 of Classical Revival, see page 178. Photo by Gareth McCormack - garethmccormack.com.

BELSHADE BUTTRESS

There are plenty of good single-pitch routes on the smaller crags but the multi-pitch routes on Belshade Buttress are outstanding. Descend via the rocky hillside east of the crag.

The following three routes are approached by padding up the 60m long rib of slabby rock at around VD.

1 **Byzantium** VS (4c,4c,4c,4a,4b)   122m

The lower section gives some very good climbing, but the upper part is somewhat rambling.
P1   17m Climb the clean corner, moving left onto a vegetated ledge at 14m, then up right to belay.
P2   27m Climb the corner above, moving left at the top. Climb diagonally right and up past vegetation to the large block on the wall on the left.
P3   20m Move left across the block and up the groove above (crux). Follow a good crack left at the top of the groove to a ledge.
P4   28m Climb the groove above to the second of two ledges.
P5   30m Move right across the slab to a steep crack. Climb this and the groove above. Follow the rib on the right to the top.
F. Winder, P. Hill 02/08/1954

2 **Classical Revival** HVS (4c,5a,4c)   83m

A stupendous route on immaculate granite.
P1   17m As for P1 of Byzantium.
P2   38m Move up and right to the base of a heather filled corner. Step right onto the arete and airily swing round right onto the wall to a good crack. Climb this and the corner above. Follow the diagonal cracks and narrow ramp with increasing difficulty and plenty of exposure across the blank slab. Belay 5m below the roof on a small ledge beneath a good crack. See photo on page 174.
P3   28m Climb the crack swinging left past the overhang on delightful holds. Continue up the corner above and finish up the arete on the left or the awkward chimney.
D. Stelfox, U. MacPherson, I. Rea 04/04/1981

3 **Mystery Tour** E1 (4b,4c,4c,5b,5a,4c)   125m

A rising traverse of the crag from left to right.
P1   30m From the rib of rock to the right of the bottom of P1 of Byzantium, move delicately down and right across a steep wall to a corner at 3m. Climb this easily to a grassy slab leading to a grass ledge at the foot of a steep groove.
P2   30m Climb the groove on finger jams and friction and step right onto the main slab. From here delightful, easy climbing leads across the slab on the line of ledges to a grassy pulpit. It's possible to belay at the start of the slab thus allowing both leader and second to appreciate the airy situations.
P3   10m Descend for 2m and move horizontally right to the crack at the end of P1 of Lest We Forget. Follow this to the corner belay.

P4 25m Move right along the ledge and follow P2 of Midgesummer Nightmare up the rounded parallel grooves until beneath the huge block. Move right around the base of the block and follow the obvious line to the belay at the top of P2 of Land of Hearts Desire.

P5 25m As for P3 of Land of Hearts Desire.

P6 5m As for P4 of Land of Hearts Desire.

D. Stelfox, W. Brown-Kerr 10/07/1983

Approach the following routes from the sloping heather ledge that runs right across the bottom of the Main Face.

---

4 **Lest We Forget** HVS (4c,4c,5a)   75m

Great climbing in a great situation.

P1 39m Start at the ramp, 8m left of the prominent corner. Follow the ramp and small ledges at the foot of the crack system. Gain the crack and follow this with increasing difficulty to a ledge in a small corner below a large flake.

P2 18m Move up for 3m and step left onto a slab. Follow the crack above to the small perched ledge in the niche under the roof.

P3 18m Bridge around the roof to the twin cracks that split the slab. Bridge up these (crux) to a small niche. Continue up the crack to the top. Cams vital.

D. Stelfox, I. Rea 1982

---

5 **Midgesummer Nightmare** E1 (5b,5b,4c)   75m

This route takes a direct line between Lest we Forget and Land of Hearts Desire.

P1 35m Follow Lest We Forget for 7m before traversing right to the foot of a green corner. Climb the clean cracks and grooves immediately to the left of the corner, with increasing difficulty to reach the right side of the belay ledge of P1 of Lest We Forget.

P2 25m Climb the rounded grooves at the right side of the ledge, using the holds on the right of the blunt rib. Move right as the angle eases to a huge detached block. Move up the left side of this and swing out left onto the slab. Climb this to a constricted belay in a narrow corner.

P3 15m From here follow the cracks above to the edge. Move right and finish up the crack in the slab.

D. Stelfox, W. Brown-Kerr 09/07/1983

---

6 **Land of Hearts Desire** HVS (5a,5a,5a,4c)   83m

Sustained with contrasting climbing on each pitch.

P1 18m Climb the short steep wall just right of the small subsidiary corner. After 5m traverse right to the huge block at the foot of the main corner system.

P2 35m Follow the corner to a belay ledge just left of the twin cracks in the next corner above.

P3 26m Make a few moves up a small corner, then swing right to the twin cracks (crux). Jam up the cracks to the base of the final steep corner. Climb this and belay on the grassy ledge to the left.

P4 4m Finish up the short layback, then up grass and easy rock to belay well back.

I. Rea, D. Stelfox October 1981

Triversion

County Donegal
LOUGH BARRA
APPROACH **20 minutes**
ROCK **Granite**
D-S **1** - HS-HVS **2** - E1-E3 **3** - E4+ **0**

Lough Barra is that rare thing, a practically roadside mountain crag. Unfortunately many of the routes, particularly those on the Main Face, are heavily vegetated and require long approaches up difficult ground, however the following routes offer quality climbing on relatively clean rock.

CONDITIONS

The South Buttress is clean and quick to dry but the Delta and Main Faces suffer from seepage and need at least a week of dry weather to come into condition.

DIRECTIONS

From Letterkenny take the R250 west, continue on as it become the R251, after 13.5km turn left onto the R254, follow it for 17km and park beside Lough Barra. From Dungloe take the N56 south before turning left onto the R252, just before the village of Doochary make a sharp left turn onto the R254 and follow the road up the valley to park beside Lough Barra. Walk a short distance north up the road and head directly up the heather slopes to the crag.

SOUTH BUTTRESS

The clean sweep of rock right of the narrow gully. Descend by walking down the slopes to the south.

1 **Diversion** S 4a	125m

Nice climbing taking a fairly direct line up the centre of the buttress. Many variations are possible, **Triversion** S 4a shares the same start and finish.
P1   40m Follow the prominent rib and move right across slabs to a ledge.
P2   25m Climb the narrow ramp. Move right to a belay on the ledge level with the top of the vegetated ramp.
P3   30m Climb the slab on the left to a steep bulge, pull over this on good holds to arrive below the headwall.
P4   30m Finish up the steep, clean corner left of the overhang, stepping left near the top.
P. Kenny, F. Winder September 1955

DELTA FACE

The steep, clean wall is home to some tremendous routes. Descend from the top by following the stream that lies just past the northern end of the crag.

2 **Gethsemane** E2 (5c,4c,4c,4c)	84m

A fine route but been warned the second, third and fourth pitches lack protection.
P1   33m Follow the slanting groove to the roof. Make a difficult pull left over the roof to a rest below a very steep wall. Climb the crack in the wall and finish more easily.
P2   24m Climb the short layback pitch as for P3 of Larceny, but instead of traversing left go straight up to the smooth walls and climb delicately right into a scoop with the small spike runner. Move up to reach heather and easy rock which is

followed to the block belay at the top of P3 of Larceny.

P3 21m Step right and climb easily to the foot of the corner. Bridge over the first bulge, continue to the second and move right to the arete in a fine position. Make a difficult move up into a scoop and delicately back left to continue more easily up the arete to a good ledge and belay below the final short corner.

P4 6m Climb the deceptive corner to the top.

L. Griffin, M. Curran 1973
FFA A. Millar, P. Dunlop 1985

---

3 **Tears of Roy** E1 5b   25m

Exposed climbing on perfect rock. Start as for Gethsemane, but at 5m move right on good holds, around the bulging arete to a good flake. Climb airily up and left along the arete to the overhang. Traverse right under the overhang to join P2 of Larceny.
A. Millar, G. Colhoun May 1990

---

4 **The Deltoid Face** E3 6a   25m

Start just downhill of Gethsemane. Layback the diagonal crack to a flat hold at 6m. Move right around the bulge on good holds to a rest. Follow the vague arete up and slightly left on big flakes to the triangular niche in the roof. Climb directly through the apex of the niche on flat holds. Continue to a ledge. Abseil descent.
N. Grimes, R. Fenlon, A. Millar, B. Mortimer 28/10/1991

---

5 **Larceny** HS (4b,4a,4b,4a)   93m

Tricky route finding and a fair amount of vegetation but a good old-school adventure.

P1 20m As for P1 of Tarquin's Groove.

P2 20m Step down and onto the wall on the left. Traverse left to the grass ledge. Scramble up to the corner and move left around the front of the face past a sound but rocking block in a crack. Step down and traverse left to a small belay ledge.

P3 26m Layback the groove and climb the overhanging wall on the right using the crack. Move diagonally right across the slab to the triangular block lying at the foot of a steep corner.

P4 27m Move up and left to a groove. Climb the groove and finish up the walls above.

P. Kenny, C. Laracy August 1955

---

6 **Tarquin's Groove** HS (4b,4a,4a,4a,4b)   101m

The classic of the crag. Approach the start by scrambling up the grassy ramp to the rock step.

P1 20m Climb the short corner and clamber up the steep grass to the base of the black corner and the start of the good stuff.

P2 24m Climb the corner and belay at the holly tree.

P3 16m Cross the groove, climb the steep wall on the right and move left to the base of the crack.

P4 19m Follow the crack and belay on the ledge on the right beneath the roof.

P5 22m Traverse left under the roof and move back right over the bulge. Climb the slab right of the corner and finish up easier ground.

F. Winder, H. Drasdo August 1955

County Donegal

CRUIT ISLAND

APPROACH **1 minute**
ROCK **Granite**
D-S **10** - HS-HVS **6** - E1-E3 **6** - E4+ **0**

The small island of Cruit (pronounced critch) has over a dozen small granite crags.
The best crag, Albatross Zawn has a good selection of mostly easier routes with
very convenient access. And while not the best crag in the country it's a good option
when the sea is too rough to visit the other islands or when the mountain crags are
wet.

CONDITIONS

The rock is clean and quick drying, some of the routes on the left hand side are only
accessible at low tide.

ABOVE Photo by Iain Miller.

DIRECTIONS

From Dungloe head west on the R259. After 12km turn left (signposted 'An Chruit') just past the Viking House Hotel. Follow the road over the bridge onto Cruit Island. Pass a turn left marked by a stone marked 'Failte Cruit Island' and take the next turn left. Follow the narrow road for 400m and Albatross Zawn will come into view on the left.

1 **Supermarine** S 4a
2 **Fresh Fruit** E1 5b
3 **Gretel** E2 5c
4 **Albatross** E1 5c
5 **Norwegian Jumping Penguin** E1 5b

6 **Best Possible Taste** HS 4b
7 **Downward Facing Dog** VS 4c
8 **Saco** VD
9 **Tom's Dinner** VD
10 **Bren's Brunch** HS 4b
11 **The High Tide Alternative** S 4a
12 **High and Dry** S 4a
13 **Safe and Sound** VS 4b
14 **Flying Doctor** HS 4a
15 **The Flake** S 4a
16 **Raising Sand** S 4b
17 **Seagull** S 4a
18 **Slither Chimney** VD
19 **Crackn Slab** S 4a
20 **Ecopunk** HVS 5a
21 **Don't Call Me Rooney** E1 5c
22 **Capt. Birdseye's Reactilites** E1 5b

County Donegal

OWEY ISLAND
APPROACH **45 minutes**
ROCK **Granite**
D-S **0** - HS-HVS **1** - E1-E3 **1** - E4+ **3**

Owey is a small uninhabitable island that lies just 500m off the northwest tip of Cruit Island. Over the years many routes in the low to mid grades have been climbed but recent development has concentrated on the bigger cliffs on the northwest of the island. These cliffs, which are up to 80m tall, offer some of the most impressive climbing terrain in Ireland with striking cracks and immense overhangs. The island is well worth a visit if you are looking for adventure and there is plenty of scope for new routes, of all grades. An 80m abseil rope is required to access the routes listed here.

It's possible to camp on the island, the best spot is near the harbour or check out www.oweyhomestay.com for accommodation.

CONDITIONS

The rock dries quickly and often the weather is much better on the island than it is on the mainland. If the sea is rough it can be impossible to access the start of many routes.

DIRECTIONS

Dan Gallagher (086 6013893) takes people over to Owey from Cruit (see directions on page 184) on his boat. From the harbour on Owey walk west into the village and follow the track that leads northwest across the island to the lake.

HOLY JAYSUS WALL

From the lake climb the hill to the west moving up to a col. Drop down towards the sea, the wall is in the huge square chasm. Abseil down the middle of the wall, swinging over to the ledge on the left arete. A runner placed in the ramp at the end of the first pitch will keep you close to the wall and make it easier to reach the ledge.

| 1 **The Second Coming** E7 (5c,6b) | 45m |

Steep, sustained and very pumpy. See photo on the front cover.
P1   15m From the ledge hand traverse right for a few meters then climb a crack straight up passing a break. Belay on the vague shelf.
P2   30m Move left to the black streak, follow it directly and continue up the cracks leading from top of the streak. Near the top move left to a ledge just below and left of the highest point.
J. McCune, P. Swail 29/06/2014

FACING PAGE Photo by Craig Hiller.

2 **Immaculata** E7 (6b,6b)   50m

Climb the right hand line up the stunning overhanging wall.

P1   20m From the ledge hand traverse right across the wall for about 5m passing a spike runner. Hard moves on crimps lead up to a darker band of rock. Belay at the second horizontal break.

P2   30m Move left into the base of a good crack. Follow this to where it widens in a vague niche and move 1m right into another niche. Follow the twin parallel cracks above the niche directly to the top.

J. McCune, R. Brown 23/06/2014

THE NOSE ZAWN

To the right of the lake is some high ground which is the top of the zawn. Abseil down the black slab on the west side of the zawn to a large non-tidal platform at the base.

3 **An Sron Tochassach** E6 (6a,5b,6b)   80m

A magnificent route that weaves its way around the immense overhangs.

P1   35m Start from the left end of the ledge and climb the diagonal crack. Follow cracks and grooves straight up to a small niche under the right side of the massive triangular roof. Traverse up and left on small edges. Place a few cams under the roof and gain the arete on the left. Pull round the arete via an exhilarating move to a wonderful belay ledge/cave.

P2   8m A beautifully exposed traverse (careful rope management required). Traverse right onto the hanging slab using small holds and undercuts in the roof. Step down to the arete of the incredible hanging nose and belay a leg either side.

P3   37m Follow the steep splitter crack with increasing difficulty until it's possible to move back left to some good ledges. Soak up the exposure before attacking the strenuous overhanging exit groove.

J. McCune, K. Kilroy August 2013

4 **The Donkey's Pelvis** HVS (4c,4c)   60m

The line of least resistance.

P1   45m Climb a fine crack to a niche and a rightward trending ramp. Follow the ramp for about 4m before climbing the wall via grooves and flutings. Trend right, then up a groove to a big ledge.

P2   15m Follow the crack above the ledge to the exit groove which is blocked by a huge chockstone. Pass the chockstone on the right with care.

J. McCune, K. Kilroy August 2013

5 **The Donkey Jumped Over The Moon** E2 5b   15m

An exhilarating variation to the second pitch of The Donkey's Pelvis. From the right end of the belay ledge climb a crack with difficulty into a groove barred by a roof. Escape right under the stepped roofs on undercuts and small footholds. When they run out make a sensational move to a magnificent hold on the arete. Follow the jugs to glory.

K. Kilroy, J. McCune August 2013

TWIN CAVE BUTTRESS   MAIN WALL   NARROW ZAWN   INLAND CRAG   GRIPPLE WALL

County Donegal

GOLA ISLAND

APPROACH **45 minutes**
ROCK **Granite**
D-S **4** - HS-HVS **9** - E1-E3 **9** - E4+ **4**

The sea cliffs and outcrops of the small uninhabited island of Gola, which lies a short distance off the coast of northwest Donegal, are home to over 200 single-pitch routes. The rock is very rough, clean granite that features an abundance of breaks and cracks, so a good selection of cams is useful. Most routes are accessed by abseil so an abseil rope is essential (and a rope protector, the rock is very abrasive).

The selection here focuses on the areas where there is the greatest density of quality climbing but there are plenty of other good routes scattered across the island.

If staying overnight then camping is the only option, the best spot is between the sandy beach and the lough on the west side of the island. Please don't leave any rubbish on the island. There is a water tap at the pier.

CONDITIONS

The routes on the sea cliffs require a calm sea, when a big sea is running the two inland crags are the best option. It's not unusual for the sun to shine on the island while the mainland is shrouded in cloud and rain.

DIRECTIONS

Jimmy Sweeney (087 6607003) will ferry climbers over to Gola. And once on the island it's only a short walk to the climbing.

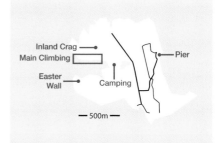

Inland Crag
Main Climbing
Easter Wall
Camping
Pier
— 500m —

FACING PAGE David Flanagan on Pride of Gola S 4a (see page 200). Photo by Michael O'Dwyer.

TWIN CAVE BUTTRESS

Twin Cave Buttress gets the sun earlier in the day than the Main Wall. Access is by abseil. A calm sea is required if your belayer is to stay dry.

1 **Kept Woman** D   20m

Lovely climbing up the series of left slanting flakes and cracks.
D. Flynn, R. Laffan 02/06/1996

2 **Asgard** E1 5b   24m

Follow the crack to the right hand side of the triangular roof. A hard move passing the roof on its right leads to good holds out left. Finish more easily up the slab.
M. Daly, S. McMullan September 1996

3 **Cois Farraige** HVS 5a   24m

Sustained and well protected jamming up the crack.
P. Breen, S. McMullan 02/06/1996

4 **Jolly Hockey Sticks** E4 6b   25m

Good strenuous climbing but should be avoided if there are birds nesting on the ledge. Climb up to the corner, the crux is just before the roof. Yard through the middle of the roof and finish directly above.
A. Sarhan, J. Gernon Summer 1999

5 **Flake Out** VS 5a   25m

Easy climbing after a hard start. Move up towards the base of the wide crack, step right to the groove and follow the left side of the groove to the top.
P. Breen, S. McMullan 29/06/1996

MAIN WALL

The Main Wall is home to the greatest concentration of quality routes on Gola. Access the base by abseiling down the corner between Galway Hooker and Snow Desert, alternatively at low tide it's possible to climb down the stepped staircase (**Descent Route** D) at the southern end of the wall and scramble along the base.

6 Gathering Momentum E5 5c   25m

Steep, sustained and safe. Follow the crack to the faint corner/groove. Continue up this and leave it to finish slightly rightward, avoiding the obvious soft left hand finish.
R. Browner, S. Coughlan 03/08/1996

Cormorant Crack

7 **Central Route** E4 6a

25m

Follow the wide, hanging groove and narrow chimney with increasing difficulty to the cracks. Continue strenuously up the leftward-trending crack on good jams to finish.
K. Pyke, A. Anderson 25/08/1997

8 **Hyperglide** E3 6a

25m

Bridge easily up the dark corner until it becomes too wide. Swing left into the crack, and follow it to the top.
R. Browner, S. Coughlan 03/08/1996

9 **Run of the Arrow** VS 4b

25m

A truly great route, steep and well protected. Belay on the ledges just right of the corner and step left into the corner which is followed to the top. See photo on page 196. **Cormorant Crack** HS 4b shares the same start but follows the crack up the left wall.
P. Harrington, A. Romero May 1996

Abseil

Descent Route

10 **Ceol na Mara** E2 5c   25m

Follow Run of the Arrow for 5m before moving right to the arete which is followed to the ledge. Climb the thin crack above the right end of the ledge to the larger ledge above and finish more easily up the crack.
P. Breen, S. McMullan 02/06/1996

11 **Tir na Nog** E3 5c   25m

Strenuous climbing up the crack that runs up the middle of the steep wall.
M. Daly, P. McGarrity 02/06/1996

12 **Galway Hooker** E4 6a   25m

Climb the crack strenuously with a difficulty move to the ledge at 10m. Continue to a rest at the small niche before a steep finish on rounded holds.
M. Daly, P. McGarrity 15/06/1996

13 **Snow Desert** HS 4b   25m

Climb the cracks and grooves up the middle of this wall.
P. Harrington, A. Romero May 1996

14 **Constitution** E4 6a   25m

Start up the wide crack before following the narrow crack up and left to the arete.
P. Breen, P. Harrington 30/06/1996

15 **Ship Wrecked** E2 5b   15m

Easy climbing leads to awkward moves getting established in the sentry box. Continue up the grooves above to the top.
P. Breen, P. Harrington, S. MacGearailt 02/09/1995

16 **Destitution** E2 5b   15m

Great steep climbing on good holds and bomber gear. Follow the crack to the niche. Move right and up a flake to a ledge and finish up the grooves.
P. Breen, S. McMullan, P. Harrington June 1996

17 **Cornered Rats** HVS 5b   15m

Interesting but awkward climbing up the corner.
M. McInerney, D. Doyle

18 **Born Again Climber** E1 5b   15m

Fantastic climbing up the steep wall just right of the square roof. Climb the crack with hard moves, past the overlap. Make committing moves up and right before trending left on slopey holds to the top.
S. MacGearailt, T. O'Brien 02/09/1995

To the east is the stepped staircase of the **Descent Route** D.

FACING PAGE Patrick Connally on Run of the Arrow VS 4b (see page 195). Photo by Jeremy Colandairaj.

NARROW ZAWN

The west side of Narrow Zawn forms an impressive, steep wall. The rock mightn't be quite as good as that on the Main Wall due to it's sheltered position but there is plenty of atmosphere. Approach by abseil.

19 **The Green Pool** E1 5b   17m

Belay on a ledge just right of the crack at low tide, or take a hanging belay 2m above. Climb the crack, passing the overlap with difficulty (crux) and continuing up the corner to the top.
M. Daly, P. McGarrity 15/06/96

20 **Buzz Light Year** HS 4b   14m

Abseil to the ledge and follow the groove on the right to the top.
C. Torrans, C. Sheridan 29/06/96

THIS SPREAD Nina Sefcikova on The Green Pool E1 5b. Photo by Juraj Navratil.

GRIPPLE WALL

A great selection of easier routes. Abseil to the ledge system at base of the wall.

21 **Muin na Muice** D
20m

The diagonal line of cracks. **Gripple Wall** VD climbs the higher line to the right.
D. Flynn, R. Laffan 02/06/1996

22 **Jean A Cheval** S 4a
20m

Classic/horrific chimney climbing. **Sea Eagle** HS 4b finishes up the corner on the right.
J. McCann, B. Forde, P. Roach 02/06/1996

23 **Who Gets the Credit?** HVS 5a
20m

Steep climbing between ledges leads to the small overlap and an easier finish.
Unknown

24 **Ex Eagle/Big Trip/Island Life** VS 4c
20m

A sustained start leads to the overlap and easier climbing up the shallow groove.
A. Tees, B. Johnston 17/06/1995

25 **Maid of Gola** HS 4b
20m

The crack system just left of and parallel to Pride of Gola.
A. Tees, B. Johnston 17/06/1995

26 **Pride of Gola** S 4a
20m

Beautiful. Traverse right from the ledge to the base of crack which leads to the top.
See photo on page 190.
A. Tees, B. Johnston 17/06/1995

INLAND CRAG

The compact buttress north of the Main Wall is popular and has a good selection of short routes. The setting is a little tame compared to the sea cliffs but it's the best option when the sea is rough.

1 **Days of Wine and Roses** E1 5a
2 **Get Off the Bandwagon** VS 4a
3 **Weathered Window** HS 4b
4 **Tasty Morsel** HVS 5a
5 **Fast and Bulbous** HVS 5b
6 **Tongue Job** E1 5b
7 **Corner Boy** HS 4b
8 **Days of Wonder** VS 5a
9 **Early Bird** E3 6a
10 **Winds of Change** E3 6a
11 **Legislator** S 4a
12 **Fur Burger** E1 5a
13 **Gorgonzolla** E2 5c
14 **Pigs Garden** S 3c

Another bad weather option is Easter Wall which lies at the end of the headland south of the main climbing areas. The wall is short but there are plenty of routes, with the easier lines following the cracks while the harder routes venture up the blank slabs in between.

INISHOWEN

Inishowen peninsula in the northeast of Donegal is home to nearly 500 routes spread across over a dozen crags. And while none of the crags are major destinations in their own right, there is plenty of climbing, especially in the low to mid grades. The following are a few route suggestions.

MALIN HEAD

Lizard Line VD
Dawson's Diedre S 4a

DUNOWEN

Rumdoodle S 4a
Bunratti Pillar HVS 5b

DUNMORE HEAD

Diversion HS 4b
Orange Blossom HS 4b
Grecians Gift VS 4c
Shining Cossacks HVS 5a
Master of Puppets HVS 5b
Wall Rock Alterations E1 5b
10CC E1 5b
Thank You and Goodbye E3 6a
Ruthless People E4 6b

KINNEGO BAY

Forked Lightening VS 4c
Austin's Window E1 5b
Atlantic Ocean Wall E4 6a

Check the references on page 285 for further information.

THIS PAGE Kevin Kilroy on Atlantic Ocean Wall E4 6a. Photo by Jeremy Colandairaj.

County Antrim
FAIR HEAD
APPROACH **20-45 minutes**
ROCK **Dolerite**
D-S **0** - HS-HVS **8** - E1-E3 **26** - E4+ **7**

Fair Head is undoubtedly the best crag in Ireland. The long arc of dolerite extends for 3km and is home to over 400 routes. The longest routes are just over 100m long but there's plenty of single-pitch routes as well. The rock is steep and there are very few routes below VS. And while there is plenty to keep the VS/HVS climber busy for a few days, to get the most out of the crag you need to be climbing in the Es.

There is a massive number of classic routes, the majority feature some variety of well protected crack or corner climbing, however some of the harder routes venture onto the blank walls where protection may be a little sparse. The climbing is sustained, good jamming, laybacking, chimneying and bridging skills make life a little easier.

The crag can be intimidating, especially in the more remote, darker areas in the middle but this just adds to the atmosphere of this unique cliff.

The selection of routes in this chapter is only the tip of the iceberg and I recommend that anyone who is planning an extended visit purchases a copy of the 2014 Mountaineering Ireland guidebook.

Bring as much gear as you can, hexes, double sets of cams and nuts. The rock is reasonably solid especially on the most popular routes but a helmet is still a good idea. As walking along the base of the crag can be slow and dangerous, an abseil rope, ideally 100m, is a very useful piece of equipment.

THIS SPREAD David Ewing on Burn Up HVS (5a,5a), Grey Man's Path (see page 213). Photo by Pedro Pimentel.

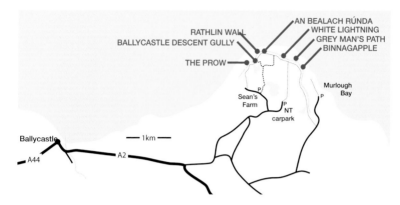

CONDITIONS

In theory it's possible to climb at the Head all year round, but as the crag faces north it gets no sun in the winter and is very cold. However in the warmer months the Prow and Rathlin Wall (which face west and northwest respectively) get plenty of sun later in the day. Seepage isn't usually a problem and the rock dries reasonably quickly after rain especially on the cleaner, more popular routes.

DIRECTIONS

There are two parking options, Sean's carpark which is best for the more western areas (The Prow, Ballycastle Descent Gully, Rathlin Wall, An Bealach Rúnda) and the National Trust carpark which is best for the eastern end (White Lightning, Grey Man's Path, Binnagapple).

Follow the M2 north out of Belfast and turn onto the A26, 15km past Ballymena turn right onto the A44 (signposted 'Ballycastle'). Drive through Ballycastle, turn right at the roundabout and take the next turn left onto the A2. After a few miles turn left at the Hunter's Bar and take the first turn left (signposted 'Fair Head Car Park'). Continue straight on to the end of the road for the National Trust carpark, for Sean's turn left after 2km, the carpark is on the right after 500m, just past the farm buildings.

To access the Ballycastle Descent Gully from Sean's carpark walk through the gates to the left of the farm buildings and follow the track for 10 minutes to the edge of the lake. Skirt around the shore of the lake to the point nearest the cliff.

For Grey Man's Path follow a way-marked path out of the National Trust carpark, go through the gate, over a stile, and across the heather to the cliff, then turn right and follow the path to the top of The Grey Man's Path.

FACING PAGE Jeremy Colandairaj on P2 of Griona VS (4c,4c) (see page 228). Photo by René Caroline Temple.

BINNAGAPPLE

The most easterly part of the Main Crag lies between an extensive vegetated area to the east and Grey Man's Path to the west. It gets the sun early in the morning.

The most common approach is to descend the Grey Man's Path gully and carefully walk along the base of the crag. Alternatively park at Murlough carpark, follow the track to the boulders and scramble up to the base. The final option is to abseil (100m rope required). There is an abseil block set back from the cliff edge at the top of Hurricane.

1 **December** HVS (4c,5a)   55m

The delicate first pitch is followed by a strenuous second pitch.
P1   25m Climb the corner and belay at the niche (#4 cam useful for belay).
P2   30m Continue up the corner, passing a ledge, and pulling on good holds through the overhang.
P. McHugh, J. McKenzie December 1968

2 **Hurricane** E2 (5b,5b)
61m

A classic route with sustained and exposed climbing.

P1 37m Follow the groove to the overlap at 12m. Cross the overlap (crux) on good fist jams and continue up the steep crack to a good belay on the left.

P2 24m Climb up to the overlap and hand traverse left along the crack on small footholds and continue up the left-hand crack to the top. Alternatively climb straight through the overlap (5c), move slightly left to good jugs and finish up the steep crack.

P. McHugh, H. O'Brien June 1969
FFA C. Torrans, C. Sheridan 1974
Direct finish - G. Somerville, R. Hunt 17/07/2006

3 **Toby Jug** E1 (5a,5b)   49m

This route has a brilliant second pitch featuring steep exposed jamming.
P1 27m Climb the crack weaving left then right before joining the main crack which is followed with difficulty to the belay ledge.
P2 22m Continue up the crack to the small roof and move left to the foot of the leaning corner which is climbed on excellent jams.
C. Torrans, R. Cowan 1970
FFA C. Torrans, C. Sheridan 1976

4 **The Brasser** E2 (5c,5b)   46m

Excellent climbing on both pitches, hard for the grade.
P1 36m Climb the corner passing a good spike runner on the left. Continue with increasing difficulty to the foot of the groove. Layback the crack and pull into the groove. Continue up the crack, initially on poor jams to the belay ledge.
P2 10m Layback the corner to ledge. Awkward finish.
C. Torrans, C. Sheridan 08/10/1978
FFA K. Murphy 11/06/1983

5 **Sandpiper** E2 (5c,5a)   44m

A great route on fantastic rock.
P1 36m Follow The Brasser to the groove and make a hard step right to the finger cracks on the right wall. Follow these cracks, which get wider, to a belay on the ledge.
P2 8m Climb the wide crack to the top.
C. Torrans, C. Sheridan 12/03/1976
FFA R. Lawson 1980

6 **Jolly Roger** E3 (6a,5c)   57m

A superb route and reasonable for the grade.
P1 27m Climb up to a small overhang and pass it on the right using good holds. Step left and up to the thin crack which is climbed with increasing difficulty to a good jug. Continue more easily to a small ledge.
P2 30m Sustained. Follow the crack passing a few bulges.
M. Manson, J. Codling 11/09/1981
FFA E. Cooper, M. McNaught 19/12/1981

7 **Track of the Cat** E4 6a   45m

Sustained wall climbing, watch out for the sting in the tail! Climb the thin crack directly to the short leaning corner and final bulge.
J. Codling, G. Gibson 28/06/1985

GREY MAN'S PATH

The steep, narrow gully known as Grey Man's path allows easy access on foot to the middle of the crag. As the rock faces due north it can get quite cold and is slow to dry.

8 **Burn Up** HVS (5a,5a)   75m

A classic and hard for the grade (some say E1). See photo on page 205.
P1 39m Climb the groove passing the steep bulge (awkward). Belay on the left 10m past the bulge.
P2 36m Reserve a #4 cam for the final moves. Continue up the crack with increasing difficulty until a big ledge is reached on the right (optional belay). Step back into the crack and layback to the top.
P. McHugh, S. Billane June 1970

WHITE LIGHTNING AMPHITHEATRE

West of The Grey Man's Path is a spectacular amphitheatre. Either walk over very rough ground from Grey Man's or abseil (100m rope required) from the block at the top of Hallowe'en.

9 **Born to Run** E4 (6a,5c,5c)   81m

One of the best routes in the country.
P1   32m Climb the wall and corner until it's possible to move right to a flake, use this to gain the overhang. Climb the overhang and continue up the crack for 10m passing two small ledges, belay on the third.
P2   20m Follow the crack until it's possible to step left and up to a ledge, then follow a series of small ledges to a semi-hanging belay.
P3   29m Climb the sustained finger crack and follow the diagonal fault right to a groove. Climb the groove with some difficulty and move right to a ledge. Move up to a higher ledge and follow good holds to a ledge just below the top. Finish easily.
E. Cooper, M. Manson 11/06/1982
FFA K. Murphy 28/08/1982

10 **Hallowe'en** E4 (5c,6a,4c)   85m

Two excellent pitches, reasonable for the grade.
P1   30m Step off the flake and climb the left wall of the corner, move left to a small roof and climb this using the crack to a good ledge.
P2   45m Follow the crack passing two ledges and continue up (sustained) until the crack starts to run out level with a small clean ledge on the left. Make some technical moves left to the ledge. Continue up to the slabby corner above.
P3   10m Climb the corner.
E. Cooper, P. Nolan 31/10/1985

AN BEALACH RÚNDA AREA

This remote part of crag contains one of Fair Head's best routes. Scramble down Ballycastle Descent Gully and follow the faint path east to the distinctive detached pillar (takes 25 minutes). Alternatively abseil down the wall just to the east (100m rope required).

11 **An Bealach Rúnda** E1 (5a,5b,5a)   105m

A stunning route, full of atmosphere.
P1 45m Climb the crack and chimney to a ledge at 12m. Move up left to climb the crack between the main column and the wall, chimney up, passing a ledge on the right at 36m. Continue up with a slight increase in difficulty to a good ledge on the right.
P2 30m Move up and left airily to the top of the detached column and flake. Cross the flake to the wall, an awkward move up the wall brings jugs and a ledge on the right. Climb the short wall on the left (crux) and continue up the thin crack to the ramp. Easier climbing leads to a large ledge. Climb a short, awkward groove to exit right onto a large ramp, move back left to a good ledge.
P3 30m Climb the ramp and make an awkward move left to small ledges. Go up right to a corner crack, follow this to a ledge (optional belay) and finish up the crack in the final steep wall.
C. Torrans, C. Sheridan 15/01/1976

RATHLIN WALL

Rathlin Wall consists of a long sequence of corners, aretes and walls east of the Ballycastle Descent Gully. With a huge number of starred routes and easy access it's the most popular area at the Head. Its northwesterly aspect means that it gets good sun during the afternoon and evenings.

The routes are described from left to right as you face the rock. Approach either by descending Ballycastle Descent Gully and walking east along the path or by abseiling directly down your chosen route. The grassy notch between the huge boulder and the cliff marks the start of the following two routes.

12 **Roaring Meg** VS (5a,4b,4a)   100m

A good route with a great first pitch however the finish is a little scrappy.
P1   35m Climb the rightward-slanting crack passing the overhang on the left.
P2   35m Follow the crack to the ramp on the right. Climb the ramp easily until the crack narrows and steepens giving an awkward move before the belay.
P3   30m Climb the corner and traverse the long narrow shelf to the final corner which requires care.
C. Torrans, J. Magennis September 1975

13 **Cúchulainn** E2 (5b,5c,5c)   77m

High quality climbing at the top of the grade.
P1   33m Climb the crack until a move left can be made onto small ledges, then move up and back into the crack (difficult). Continue up the crack (sustained) to a recess and a short offwidth crack. Gain the sloping edge and continue up the crack to belay on large flakes.
P2   21m Gain the ramp above the belay. Move back left into the corner and crack. Climb the crack to the overhang and move out left over this to a small shelf - good jamming. Climb a few feet to a thin crack with a groove on the right. Bridge up the crack and groove to another overhang. Climb this on good jams to reach yet another small shelf. Belay below an undercut offwidth crack.
P3   23m Climb the crack passing a jammed block (strenuous) with increasing difficulty to a ledge at the foot of a grassy groove which leads to the top.
C. Torrans, C. Sheridan 22/10/1977

14 **The Hustler** E3 (5c,6a)   58m

Brilliant airy climbing. The first pitch is shared with Cool Hand Luke.
P1   28m Follow the groove until it's possible to step right onto a delicate ramp. Climb directly up the wall above (just to the right of a flake crack) to a small ledge. Move right for 2m and climb the wall to a crack with a downward-pointing spike. Continue up the crack to a good belay ledge.
P2   30m Climb the wall directly above the belay to a small sloping ledge on the arete just below a short steep groove. Move left, then back right into the groove (or climb the groove direct at 6b) and finish up the brilliant crack.
E. Cooper, J. McDonald 07/06/1986

15 **Conchubair** E2 (5a,5c)   58m

An intimidating route featuring good sustained climbing. Scramble up to the start of the route from the left.

P1 25m Climb the corner to a ledge on the left and belay (semi-hanging) in the corner crack on good footholds, just above the small ledge.

P2 33m Continue up the corner with increasing difficulty to a rest near the top. Move left on a good foothold to a thin crack. Follow this to the overhang (crux). Climb the overhang using good holds to a V chimney. Finish up this exiting left near the top.

K. Higgs, T. Ryan 13/04/1980

16 **Face Value** E4 (6a,6a)   80m

Sensational climbing, one of the easier E4s at the Head. The second pitch follows Flying Lizards. See photo on page 220.

P1 40m Scramble in from the left over grass and blocks to a roof and thin crack. Climb the crack to a rocking jug and continue up to the recess (#3 cam). Climb this and the thin cracks above until forced right onto a small shelf. From here move up and left and continue up to a belay on good footholds beneath the roof.

P2 40m Traverse left for about 5m and climb the wall to the overhang and short corner on the left. Climb the overhang with a long reach to a good jug, then step right for a rest and runners, before trending back left, with difficulty, to a groove. Climb this to a second band of overhangs which are negotiated with good jugs first on the right, then on the left. Easier climbing leads to the top.

E. Cooper, S. McCrory June 1986

17 **Primal Scream** E5 (5b,6b)   60m

A beautiful, serious pitch.

P1 24m As for P1 of Blind Pew.

P2 36m From the belay traverse left to a peg. Follow the obvious line (runners are poor and difficult to find, but improve after about 20m) to a small ledge, from here gain a blind flake above (crux) and continue more easily with improving runners to a horizontal break. From the horizontal break follow the left hand right-trending crack to the top.

E. Cooper, A. Moles Spring 1992

18 **Blind Pew** E2 (5b,5b)   57m

A great route, one of the easier E2s at Fair Head.

P1 24m Climb the corner to a belay ledge.

P2 33m Continue up the leaning corner (holds improve after 9m) to a delicate scoop. Move up this to the base of two grooves, step into the right-hand groove and follow it with increasing difficulty to the top.

K. Higgs, E. Goulding 28/10/1978

19 **Mizen Star** E2 (5b,5b)   60m

Well protected jamming on the first pitch and bold, face climbing on the second..
P1 39m Follow the short groove and crack to a flake. Make a hard move up the
flake to good holds. Move right to the base of the crack. Jam up the crack, passing
the overlap using a good jug on the right, to a narrow ledge. Move left to a belay.
P2 21m Step left and climb the arete on flat edges, before making bold moves
right to the groove. Climb the groove to an overlap with a chockstone. Pass this on
the left and climb the crack, finishing up easy but doubtful-looking rock.
C. Torrans, C. Sheridan 03/09/1977

20 **Titanic** E2 (5b,5c)   53m

A technical first pitch and strenuous second. The hardest of the trio of E2s?
P1 21m Climb the deep groove with delicate moves at 8m, continue over a small
bulge and more easily to a steep finger crack. Follow this to a ledge on the left.
P2 32m Step back right and climb the steep crack to a rest below the bulge.
Layback over the bulge (crux, #5 cam useful) to a sharp crack. Follow the crack to
a ledge and continue up the crack to a rocking chockstone. Difficult climbing leads
to good footholds on the left. Continue over a bulge on a good hold to a ledge and
finish up the short, steep crack.
K. Higgs, T. Ryan 22/10/1977
FFA P. Livesey, C. Torrans 1977

FACING PAGE Damian O'Sulllivan on P1 of Face Value E4 (6a,6a) (see page 219). Photo by Richard Creagh.

21 **Salango** E3 (5b,5c)   60m

A compelling line with considerable exposure towards the top of the second pitch.
P1   36m Climb easily up the groove to an awkward step up and then left to a sloping ledge under the overhang. Climb the overhang on good jams to a finger crack which is followed with difficulty to a belay under the next overhang.
P2   24m Climb through the overhang to a steep crack, follow the crack (crux) to a groove. Move up the groove to an overhanging flake and make a difficult move over the overhang to good jugs and the top.
C. Torrans, C. Sheridan, J. Tasker 21/11/1976
FFA P. Livesey, K. Higgs 1977

22 **Equinox** E2 (5b,5b)   58m

Sustained climbing up the huge corner. Often climbed in a single pitch.
P1   37m Bridge up the corner, passing the overlap, belay at a small stance just above.
P2   21m Continue up the corner, pass the bulge using good jugs which lead to the top.
P. McHugh, S. Billane 27/03/1970
FFA C. Torrans, C. Sheridan 1977

FACING PAGE Sean Villanueva O'Driscoll on Where the Grass is Green E7 6c (see page 224). Photo by Ben Ditto.

The steep wall taken by the following two hard classics is also home to an incredible collection of even harder three-star routes including **A Bad Skin Day** E7 6c, **The Big Skin** E8 6c, **The Rathlin Effect** E8 6c, **Below and Behold** E7 6c, **Where the Grass is Green** E7 6c (see photo on page 222), **Once You Go Black You Never Go Back** E7 6c, **Taming the Tiger** E6 6b, **Way of the Jive Monkeys** E7 6b, **Styx** E7 6b.

23 **Above and Beyond** E6 (6b,6b)   65m

Bold, strenuous climbing of the highest calibre. The runners are mainly small nuts.
P1 30m As for P1 of The Wall of Prey.
P2 35m Step left onto a narrow ledge, move left and up to a good hold. Make a rising traverse to the left for 10m where hard moves lead to a sloping ledge below a steep wall and a peg (not great). Climb the steep wall to a ledge beneath the final groove. Move right and up the groove to good finishing holds.
P. Littlejohn, E. Cooper 28/05/1984

An impressive line up the middle of the wall.

P1   30m Follow the groove until it's possible to move right to a thin crack near the arete. Continue to the roof passing a peg. Cross the roof at a small jammed block, gain the groove above and move right to a hanging belay.

P2   30m Climb the right-hand crack, stepping into the left one for a few moves until forced back right. Climb the bulge above until sloping holds allow access to the top.

A. Strapcans, G. Jenkins 31/08/1979

Following rockfall - C. Torrans, C. Sheridan 1996

BALLYCASTLE DESCENT GULLY EAST

Popular and very convenient. Descend carefully down the gully, the following routes are on the wall to your right.

25 **Hell's Kitchen** HVS (5a,5a)   66m

A good route with a brilliant, exposed finish.
P1   36m Start up the wall just left of the corner before moving right and climbing the corner to a small ledge.
P2   30m Continue up the corner until a delicate step up can be made to a good finishing hold on the right.
J. McKenzie, D. Richardson September 1974

26 **Ocean Boulevard** E3 (5c,5b)   60m

An awesome route with a sustained, technical first pitch.
P1   39m Climb to the base of the narrow groove. Climb the groove and crack with increasing difficulty to a small ledge.
P2   21m Climb the blocky corner until it's possible to step right around the arete to the corner which is followed to the top.
C. Torrans, T. Irving 21/06/1978

27 **Aoife** E2 (5b,5a)   57m

Exposed, acrobatic climbing.
P1   32m Take the groove to a steep corner, climb the corner and pull through the steepness using the flakes to a rest below the crack. Follow the crack with increasing difficulty to a good ledge.
P2   25m Climb the wall behind the belay to a short ramp and corner which are followed to easier ground.
C. Torrans, C. Sheridan October 1976

28 Girona VS (4c,4c) 47m

A great mix of climbing in a spectacular setting, tough for the grade.
P1 27m Follow the short groove to the overhang. Climb this on the right and make a hard move back left to the crack (crux). Continue up the crack trending slightly right past dubious blocks to the ledge right of the pillar.
P2 20m Chimney up behind the pillar and climb the wall above over a series of ledges. See photo on page 206.
S. Billane, C. Torrans May 1976

29 Chieftain VS (4b,4b) 54m

More brilliant climbing but not quite as hard as Girona.
P1 28m Climb the deep left-facing groove for 4m before moving right onto the arete. Make a thin move up the arete to good holds. Move up and left to the ledge.
P2 26m Follow the crack to the base of a groove. Get into the groove using good jugs and follow it to the top.
C. Torrans, D. Mitchell 01/12/1974

THE PROW

Most first time visitors head straight to the Prow, its shorter, less intimidating single-pitch routes are a good place to get familiar with the Fair Head style of climbing. Plus the rock dries quickly and it gets good sun in the afternoons and evenings.

Approach on foot along the vague path from the base of the Ballycastle Descent Gully or down the heather slopes to the west of the crag. Alternatively abseil from the large boulders above Midnight Cruiser (one 50m required assuming you are leaving it in place).

30 **Darkness** E2 5c   44m

Excellent finger-crack climbing. Follow Mongrel Fox for 15m where you step left to the sustained, thin crack which is followed to the top.
C. Torrans, C. Sheridan 25/06/1981

31 **Mongrel Fox** E1 5b   42m

Sustained jamming. Climb the deep groove to an overhang at 10m. Climb the overhang on the left to a small niche. Jam up the twin cracks to a block, continue up the twin cracks on the right and move right to good ledges. Continue up the right-hand crack until it's possible to move left to the base of the scoop. Step right into the crack, difficult moves lead to the jammed blocks and the top.
C. Torrans, C. Sheridan 06/02/1977

32 **Thunderhips** E1 5b   39m

Follow Fireball for 7m to a small foothold on the left wall and traverse left to a good crack. Climb with increasing difficulty. See photo on page 8.
C. Torrans, S. Billane 22/02/1975

33 **Fireball** E1 5b   39m

Sustained and technical. Climb the wide crack on good jams (sustained) until large holds on the left can be reached and used to get into a deep groove. Finish up the groove with a difficult bulge near the top.
T. Ryan, K. Higgs 04/12/1976

34 **Midnight Cruiser** E1 5b   36m

Good pumpy climbing. Follow the corner up to the overlap. Once over the overlap move up to a rest on the right wall at mid-height. Continue up twin cracks (crux) to a difficult finish on flat holds.
T. Ryan, F. Nugent 18/03/1979

35 **Marconi** E3 5c   36m

Interesting face climbing. Climb the crack to a groove and follow this to a bulge (crux). Finish up the groove. See photo on facing page.
C. Torrans, C. Sheridan 04/11/1984

FACING PAGE Viliam Rentka on Marconi E3 5c. Photo by Juraj Navratil.

36 **The Embankment** E2 5c   40m

Follow Railroad until level with the small roof where you step left to the groove and follow it to the top (protection is a little sparse). See photo on facing page.
C. Torrans, C. Sheridan 02/12/1984

37 **Railroad** E1 5b   36m

A quality route. Climb the wall (delicate) to a horizontal break at 7m. Follow the crack on the right with sustained difficulty to the twin cracks and climb directly up and over the overlap on good holds and jams, finishing up the steep crack.
K. Higgs, T. Ryan 06/02/1977

38 **Fáth Mo Bhuartha** E1 5b   24m

Sustained finger jamming. Follow the crack to a good ledge. Continue up using the two cracks passing two bulges before moving up the right-hand crack. Follow the crack over the bulge (crux) to the top.
D. Somers, J. Dwyer 1977

39 **GBH** E3 6a   24m

Hard, well protected crux. Follow the crack on good jams to the bulging wall. Climb the wall on well-spaced flat holds to a small rounded foothold. Make difficult moves up the thin crack on good finger slots before a high step to a sloping foothold. Continue up the crack on good jams.
C. Torrans, C. Sheridan 10/06/1979
FFA K. Murphy 1982

40 **The Black Thief** VS 4b   24m

Welcome to Fair Head. Climb the groove, finishing up the right-hand crack.
C. Sheridan, C. Torrans 18/12/1976

41 **The Fence** VS 4c   24m

Hard for the grade. Climb the crack and groove right of The Black Thief, the crux is breaching the overhang on good jams.
C. Torrans, S. Billane 26/12/1976

FACING PAGE Ross Mathers on The Embankment E2 5c. Photo by James Dunn Visuals.

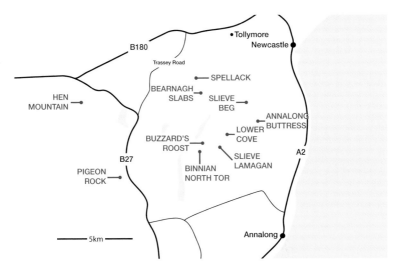

Map labels:
- Tollymore
- Newcastle
- B180
- Trassey Road
- SPELLACK
- BEARNAGH SLABS
- SLIEVE BEG
- HEN MOUNTAIN
- ANNALONG BUTTRESS
- LOWER COVE
- BUZZARD'S ROOST
- B27
- BINNIAN NORTH TOR
- SLIEVE LAMAGAN
- A2
- PIGEON ROCK
- Annalong
- 5km

MOURNES

The Mourne Mountains contain over two dozen climbing areas and more than a thousand routes. The rock is well weathered granite, sound and rough, characterised by rounded horizontal breaks and large, featureless expanses.

Most of the crags - with the exceptions of Pigeon Rock and Hen Mountain - are a decent walk from the road.

ACCOMMODATION

There is plenty of accommodation in the towns surrounding the Mournes. Newcastle to the north and Warrenpoint in the west are all good bases. www.visitmournemountains.co.uk has plenty of information about accommodation as well as things to do on rest days in the area.

Some of the more remote crags would make idea places to wild camp, making the most of the long walk-ins.

OTHER CLIMBING

There are too many crags in the Mournes to mention them all here. Eagle Rocks, Bearnagh Tor and Ben Crom all have some very worthwhile routes.

REST/RAINY DAYS

There is a number of excellent mountain biking trails in Rostrevor, and it's possible to hire bikes for a day. See www.mountainbikeni.com for details.

The nearest climbing wall is in Tollymore Outdoor Centre (www.tollymore.com) just outside Newcastle.

Check out www.walkNI.com for loads of information about walking in the Mournes.

FACING PAGE Vicki Cleary on Pillar Variant S 4a, Lower Cove (see page 266). Photo by Richard Creagh.

County Down

PIGEON ROCK
APPROACH **10 minutes**
ROCK **Granite**
D-S **1** - HS-HVS **4** - E1-E3 **4** - E4+ **0**

Pigeon is one of the most popular crags in the Mournes thanks to its short approach and good selection of single and multi-pitch routes.

CONDITIONS

East facing so it doesn't get much sun later in the day.

DIRECTIONS

From Newry follow the A2 east, turn left at the traffic lights in Kilkeel and immediately turn left again. Follow this road (B27) for 10km to a gated parking area on the left. From Newcastle take the B180 west until you meet the B27 which you follow south for 9km to the parking area. Park inside the gate and make sure to close it behind you. Follow the track across the river, before slogging up the slope to the foot of the crag.

FACING PAGE Martin Kocsis on Phantoms E1 5b (see page 243). Photo by Mike Hutton.

Virgo Ledge

THE MAIN FACE

Home to a couple of very good, recently cleaned, multi-pitch routes. Descend by walking south, crossing the fence, passing the steep, grassy gully, and carefully scrambling down the shallow gully.

1 **Virgo** VS (4c,4b,4c) — 80m

Exposed, technical climbing.
P1 25m Follow the distinctive crack to the block, step from the block to the slab and traverse steeply left (crux). A series of mantles lead to the large ledge. Belay at the left end.
P2 30m Traverse up and right of the blunt arete. Move right around the arete on a small ledge and traverse right (exposed) before climbing directly to Virgo Ledge.
P3 25m Climb the corner left of the nose.
C. Moore, H. Porter 22/04/1965

2 **Lunar Wall** E1 5b — 30m

Great climbing, well protected climbing. Climb the chimney to a ledge. Move left along the steep wall to a groove,. Follow the groove to a small triangular ledge. Move left up over a series of ledges to the Virgo Ledge. Finish up P3 of Virgo.
R. Cowan, C. Torrans 12/08/1968

3 **Penny Black** E2 (5c,5a) — 54m

Well protected steep, sustained climbing with a testing crux.
P1 30m Climb the groove to a stance. Step up to the flake at the arete and follow the shallow corner to the square-cut ledge on the arete. Move up and follow to the cracks (crux) up the wall (crux). Climb through the overlap to the Virgo Ledge.
P2 24m Scramble up the ledge to the right end of the large overhang. Traverse up and left above the overhang to the nose which is followed to the top.
R. Greene, R. Cowan 1969
FFA E. Cooper, T. Ryan 1983

GULLY WALL

At the top of Class Distinction, about 5m back and left of the edge is an anchor (check the slings and replace if needed). Abseiling from this is the most convenient descent (one 50m rope is sufficient).

4 **Class Distinction** S 4a   25m

A wonderful route, especially the upper half. Climb the narrow groove and trend left to the base of the steep corner. Bridge up the corner and follow it to the top.
S. Crymble and party 23/01/1966

5 **Rainbow Warrior** VS 4b   25m

A good direct line. Climb directly up the wall, skirting the overlap on its right.
A. Carden, P. Wells 10/08/1985

6 **Falcon** HS 4b   27m

Good climbing with an airy upper section. Watch out for rope drag. Climb the short crack and corner. Move right into the recess (crux). Continue up more easily before stepping right to the large block (optional belay). From the block step up and right around the corner onto a steep slab. Follow this right to a line of weakness that leads up and left to the top. Alternatively finish directly at VS 4c.
H. Porter, C. Moore 01/08/1965

CITROEN WALL

The following routes are on the clean slab that lies right of the gully. Descend by abseiling from the belay (one 50m rope is sufficient).

7 **Phantoms** E1 5b   25m

Superb climbing on positive holds. Start at the pair of parallel cracks. Climb with increasing difficulty up a series of steep walls interspersed by narrow ledges. The crux is the awkward mantleshelf, onto the ledge at the top. Traverse easily across the ledge to the peg belay. See photo on page 238.
E. Cooper, T. Cooper May 1984

8 **Citroen** HVS 4c   25m

A quality route, with hard won protection (tricams are useful). Climb directly up the steepening wall to a ledge just left of the belay.
D. Dick, C. Moore 25/06/1964

9 **Castrol R** E1 5b   25m

Enjoyable climbing with spaced protection. Climb over the bulge to a ledge. Move up directly to another small ledge just below the top. The crux is moving up and slightly right to the belay ledge. Finishing up the diagonal crack is a better protected alternative at HVS 5b.
R. Cowan, C. Torrans 1968

County Down

HEN MOUNTAIN
APPROACH **20 minutes**
ROCK **Granite**
D-S **3** - HS-HVS **5** - E1-E3 **9** - E4+ **0**

The rounded tors on the top of Hen Mountain are one of the most popular, and convenient venues in the Mournes. The rock is quite slabby and there are plenty of routes in the lower grades, however many of them are quite bold and it can be difficult to find belays on top.

CONDITIONS

Very exposed so can get cold when it's windy, but the rock dries quickly and midges aren't a problem as there is usually at least a breeze.

DIRECTIONS

From Newcastle take the B180 west to the B27. From Newry travel east through Hilltown onto the B27, turn right onto Sandbank Road Park and park in the carpark on the right. Follow the track opposite the carpark to a gate. From the gate walk directly up the steep, grassy slope.

THE TOWER

The west face of The Tower has a good selection of quality routes.

1 Jump Route VS 4c
15m

Bold. The shorter dyke 3m left of Escalator.
Unknown

2 Escalator D
15m

The leftward-trending line of nobbles. The steep line just to the right goes at S 4a.
Unknown

3 Asterisk E2 5b
25m

Some protection but still bold. Climb the ramp to a small ledge. Step up and left to a big pockmark. Finish airily up and right over the two pockets and the slab.
L. Griffin 1971

4 Journey Into Life E3 5c
25m

Brilliant. Not technically desperate but sustained with thoughtful protection and moves.
G. Murray, I. McEwan 05/10/1986

5 Quare Crack E2 5b
30m

A good line, hard for the grade. Small cams vital to protect the crux moves.
G. Murray 19/04/1987

6 Yeni Gol HS (4a,4a)
36m

More direct, bolder variations to the second pitch are possible at VS 4b.
P1 12m Climb the crack and traverse right to the ledge.
P2 24m Climb the blocky wall and step right to an overlap which leads to the top.
I. Anderson, S. Webb 15/11/1964

7 Whole of the Moon E2 6a
14m

Traverse along the dyke to a thread below the bulge. Surmount the bulge (crux) and the climb the slab. **Dreams of Distance** E2 5c takes a doglegged line to the left.
G. Murray, G. Henry October 1991

SUMMIT TOR

The west side of Summit Tor has plenty of slabby routes many of which are bold.

8 **Main Street** E1 5c
10m

Follow the nose to the horizontal break, step left and finish up the wall above.
G. Murray, R. Bankhead May 1988

9 **Little One** E1 5c
10m

Climb the wall right of the rib to the horizontal break and continue steeply up the wall above to a rounded finish.
G. Murray June 1995

10 **King of the Mountains** E2 6a
12m

Good climbing with reasonable protection. Follow Little One as far as the horizontal break. Traverse the break and finish up the short vertical groove.
G. Murray May 1997

11 **The One They Call the White Hair** VS 4c
10m

Start at the groove on the right of the buttress. Up the right edge of slab and step left onto the sloping ledge. Move up to the horizontal break and the short groove of King of the Mountains.
G. Murray April 1987

12 **Yak-Yak** D
25m

Start 3m to the left of the groove. Climb straight up the slabs to finish with a mantleshelf onto the top.
Unknown

13 Simplicity VD
21m

The prominent groove is a fine climb but lacks protection.
J. White November 1952

14 Athene VS 4b
15m

Very bold with a smeary crux. Follow the groove 1m right of Simplicity to a slight recess, then move straight up or move right to the thin dyke and follow this. Finish more easily up the slab above.
P. Wilson 20/09/1960

The following climbs start from the shelf.

15 Ethical Backfire E2 5b
15m

Quality climbing with less than reasonable protection. Climb the first groove and step right into the second groove.
E. Cooper 1985

16 L.A. Raider E1 5a
15m

Absorbing. Climb to the end of the slanting shelf and pad directly up the slab.
G. Murray, C. Cartwright 03/10/1986

17 Difficility VS 5a
12m

Climb the groove to the ledge and finish more easily.
Unknown

BINNIAN NORTH TOR
APPROACH **90 minutes**
ROCK **Granite**
D-S **1** - HS-HVS **4** - E1-E3 **2** - E4+ **1**

The rounded granite tors near the summit of Binnian North have a good selection of predominantly slab and crack climbs in a grand setting. There is also some beautiful bouldering on the very rough granite.

CONDITIONS

The tors are very exposed to the wind.

APPROACH

From the Carrick Little carpark follow the track passing Annalong Wood. Just beyond the river crossing is a fork in the track. Follow the left branch past Blue Lough to the Slieve Binnian/Slieve Lamagan col, and follow the track to the tor.

FACING PAGE Michael Kennedy on Electra E1 5b (see page 251). Photo by Michelle O'Loughlin.

The following routes are found on the northwest side of the Tor.

1 Lancastration VS 4c 30m

Both physical and delicate. Start up the shallow corner and follow the deep crack on the right. Traverse right around the arete and up the slab above via a large crystal pocket, finishing up the right-hand arm of the Y crack.
J. Leyland, P. Grindley 27/03/1959

2 York Street HS 4b 30m

Old school and hard for the grade but well protected.
F. Winder, C. McCormack, P. Gribbon 24/04/1955

3 Kimmage Groove S 4a 30m

Nice climbing but the upper section is runout. Climb the arete to ledge and finish up the crack in the slab above.
J. Morrison, P. Kenny 13/05/1951

The following routes are on the south side of the Tor, walk clockwise from the above routes passing some lovely bouldering and they soon come into view.

4 The Penguin on Newcastle Beach E1 5b 30m

Start at the foot of the main crack. Go up left and climb the short, bulging crack to a ledge. Finish up the thin crack on the right.
G. McGullough, C. Stewart 1981

5 Screamers VS 5a 30m

Good climbing with an early crux. Start up the short right-trending crack and then follow the flakes diagonally left, passing the diagonal crack, to a very small right-facing corner crack. Move up this and finish up the right-trending crack.
Unknown

6 **Rankin's Crack** HS 4b   12m

Nice crack climbing up the prominent corner.
Unknown

7 **I Am Not Spiderman** E4 6a   30m

Climb the arete to a ledge at 5m and move right to an awkward groove. From the top of the groove move up and right to a good hold at the end of the Electra traverse. Make hard moves left to a flake and reach for the top.
E.Cooper, A. Warnock, D. Hamill 02/04/2005

8 **Electra** E1 5b   20m

Delightful, well protected climbing. Climb the flake system to a bulge at 10m. Traverse left and make hard moves (crux) to get stood on a sloping ledge. Finish up and right. See photo on page 248.
I. Rea. G. Murray 18/10/1985

BUZZARD'S ROOST
APPROACH **60 minutes**
ROCK **Granite**
D-S **1** - HS-HVS **0** - E1-E3 **0** - E4+ **3**

The steep buttress is arguably the most impressive in the Mournes.

CONDITIONS

Seepage isn't a big problem but the crag faces northeast so it doesn't get much sun and is slow to dry.

DIRECTIONS

From the Carrick Little carpark follow the track passing Annalong Wood. Just beyond the river crossing is a fork in the track. Follow the left branch past Blue Lough and slog straight up the hill to the foot of the crag. See map on page 269.

---

1 **The Sheugh** S (3c,3c,3c)   73m

A dank but atmospheric journey to the heart of darkness.
P1   29m Follow the splitter crack in the middle of the right-hand wall, passing chockstones, belay on the titled chockstone.
P2   26m Follow cracks and breaks up and inwards.
P3   18m Wiggle on up to the top.
W. Gibson, M. McMurray 18/09/1954

---

2 **The Spirit Level** E5 (6b,6a)   52m

The best E5 in the Mournes?
P1   32m Make a rising traverse to the overhanging groove. Climb the groove and move left to the belay ledge on the arete.
P2   20m Traverse right across the face and finish more easily as for War Music.
One rest point - E. Cooper, P. McArthur September 1994

---

3 **War Music** E5 (6a,6b)   50m

Exhilarating climbing up the steep wall.
P1   20m Follow the line of weakness to the roof. With difficulty, traverse right around the roof and the arete to the small belay ledge.
P2   30m Move left and up to a short groove, left again and up to the slab above. The slab leads to another groove which forces you right to the base of a thin crack. Climb the crack (crux) and finish up easier but still interesting ground.
E. Cooper, A. Moles 1989
FFA E. Cooper, P. Nolan August 1994

---

4 **Divided Years** E9 6c   55m

The magnificent prow. See photo on page 286.
J. Dunne August 1994

Original
Finish

②

①

County Down
SLIEVE LAMAGAN
APPROACH **60 minutes**
ROCK **Granite**
D-S **1** - HS-HVS **1** - E1-E3 **0** - E4+ **0**

The low angled slabs on the south face of Slieve Lamagan contain some great multi-pitch routes, FM in particular is a classic.

CONDITIONS

Exposed but clean and quick drying.

DIRECTIONS

From the Carrick Little carpark follow the track north passing Annalong Wood. Just beyond the river crossing is a fork in the track. Take the right branch and follow it for around 700m before leaving the track and heading directly up to the distinctive white slab that marks the start of the route. See map on page 269.

1 **FM** S (3b,3b,3c,3b,3c)   160m

Wonderful granite slab climbing with two steeper sections. The original finish (VD) veered right across broken ground, the finish described here is a better, more direct alternative.
P1   35m Move over easy ground heading for the slabby layback corner. Belay at the ledge at the top of the corner.
P2   45m From the left end of the ledge move up through the overlap and belay just left of the corner in the middle of the low, steep wall.
P3   25m Climb up the corner and step left onto the sloping ledge with the assistance of a hidden handhold (crux). Follow the corner above which lies just left of the white streak. Belay at the top of the corner.
P4   40m Skirt the grass island and belay at the base of the steep corner.
P5   15m Layback the steep corner on massive holds.
R. Johnson and party 20/06/1948

2 **Arcadia** VS (3b,4c,3c,4b)   145m

A worthwhile route that is low in the grade.
P1   35m As for P1 of FM.
P2   35m Continue up the slabby corner and pad up the black slab to the base of a curving arch. Follow the arch right to the apex, cross the bulge (awkward) and head for the belay below the steep wall.
P3   50m Move diagonally left over a series of bulges. Belay below the steep wall.
P4   25m Climb the left hand of the two steep corners.
I. Rea, M. Rea, R. Bankhead 28/08/1995

To descent from the top of the slabs gain a little height before contouring around to the northwest until you reach a steep path that leads back to the foot of the slabs.

County Down
SPELLACK
APPROACH **30 minutes**
ROCK **Granite**
D-S **1** - HS-HVS **1** - E1-E3 **1** - E4+ **2**

Spellack has some serious test pieces
on the high quality rock of the main slab,
as well as some more modest challenges
including one of the best Severes in the
Mournes.

CONDITIONS

East facing so only gets the sun early
in the day but is sheltered from the
prevailing wind.

DIRECTIONS

From Newcastle drive west on the
B180, after 7.5km turn left onto the
Trassey Road (signposted 'Meelmore
Lodge'). Follow the road over the very
narrow bridge to a carpark on the left.
Alternatively park at Meelmore Lodge
(cafe, hostel and campsite) which is 2km
further up the road on the left.

Coming from Newry take the A25, then
the B8, then the B27, then the B180.
After 10km on the B180 turn right onto
Trassey Road. Continue as above.

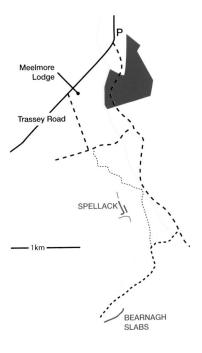

From the public carpark walk a short distance up the road, cross the stile and follow
the track through the forest. Once you reach the open hillside follow the wide path
up the valley, after 1km ford the stream on the right and walk directly up to the crag.

FACING PAGE Conor Gilmour on Blowin' in the Wind HVS 5a (see page 259). Photo by Thomas Prebble.

1 **Cabin Cruise** E1 5b
30m

Well protected, technical climbing up the prominent diagonal crack.
J. Rotherham, R. Telford, T. Haskins 13/06/1972

2 **White Walls** S 4a
30m

A Mournes classic. Scramble up the large gully left of the main face. Start below the cracked white wall at the top of the gully. Climb the slab below the wall via a series of grooves and small ledges. After reaching a large ledge on the right, step back left onto the steep wall which is climbed directly on generous holds in a very impressive situation.
R. Dean and party 1974

3 **Mad Dogs** E5 6a
35m

A long complex route, with a number of perplexing moves, and a committing run out. Start at the left end of the large grass ledge. Follow large flakes to the small overlap. Traverse right around this and move up until it's possible to traverse left under the long overlap. Move up with difficulty moves and climb the overlap to a ledge at the base of an inverted V. Step right and layback up the right-hand side of the inverted V. Make a committing series of moves (crux) up the blank wall to a second inverted V. From here, easier climbing leads to a small overlap. Swing out left of this and finish up the face.
P. Douglas, M. Manson 1980
FFA E. Cooper 02/07/1988

4 Blowin' in the Wind HVS 5a

20m

Delicate and thoughtful climbing with plenty of exposure. Climb the diagonal, sloping crack just right of the edge of the crag. See photo on page 256.

M. Manson, P. Douglas 11/05/1980

5 Warhorse E4 6a

40m

Superb face climbing. Start up the water-worn wall and follow a line of flakes diagonally right. Traverse right (peg) and up to a thread (impossible to place on lead). Then up and left to the first horizontal break (peg). Make a long reach to a flat hold below the second break. Using the pocket above the second break make a long reach up and left to a flake. Move right to another thread and continue straight up to finish. See photo on page 16.

J. Codling, P. Douglas, C. Calow 1979
FFA J. Codling 1985

County Down
BEARNAGH SLABS
APPROACH **60 minutes**
ROCK **Granite**
D-S **2** - HS-HVS **1** - E1-E3 **1** - E4+ **0**

The low angled slabs on the south side of Slieve Bearnagh have some great easy multi-pitch climbs. The rock has amazing friction and most routes have a mix of padding up blank low-angled slabs and battling up steep corners or cracks.

CONDITIONS

The slabs face northwest so they are slow to dry after wet weather.

DIRECTIONS

Follow the directions on page 257 to Spellack but continue up the wide track before taking the path up the side valley. The slabs are on the left just before the wall.

1 **Crooked Chimney** HS (3c,4b)   69m

A classic route with an 'old school' crux.
P1 37m Follow the slabby edge to a small ledge (optional belay). Move up directly to the left end of the spacious grass ledge.
P2 32m Climb left up a crack to the edge and follow the slabby rib back right to a narrow ledge below a deep corner crack (optional belay). Thrash up the crack (crux) to a small ledge (optional belay) and finish up the dogleg chimney.
S. Graham, B. Blakie, M. McMurray May 1949

2 **Grand Central** VD   70m

One of the best easy multi-pitch routes in the Mournes.
P1 35m Start at the large grass ledge and climb easily up the slabs to a grass ledge. From its left end climb the left trending groove to a right trending groove which leads to a ledge (optional belay). Climb the groove directly above for 3m before traversing left along a faint groove and up to the grass ledge shared with Crooked Chimney.
P2 35m Step down and climb diagonally right to a flake (optional belay). Move left up the slab above and finish up the awkward chimney.
Unknown

3 **Innocence** E2 (4c,5c)   60m

An excellent eliminate with a fine, bold but technically reasonable crux.
P1 25m Follow Grand Central to the first grass ledge. Move through the overlap to the left-facing corner. Climb this and move left to the belay ledge.
P2 35m Go right, but then steeply left to the groove. Follow this for 10m (crux) to a slab. Move through the bulge and finish precariously up the arete.
I. Rea, M. Rea, I. Dillon 16/05/1992

4 **Hypothesis** S (3c,4a,4a)   78m

More slabby goodness.
P1 30m Climb directly to the belay at the foot of the left-facing corner.
P2 30m Follow the diagonal crack across the slab to the belay ledge on the right.
P3 18m Finish up the crack on the left edge of the slab.
I. Firth, E. Wilkinson 1960

County Down
SLIEVE BEG
APPROACH **90 minutes**
ROCK **Granite**
D-S **1** - HS-HVS **4** - E1-E3 **4** - E4+ **0**

Slieve Beg is one of the best mountain crags in the Mournes. However it is also a little neglected and some of the routes are somewhat overgrown. The crag is split by a wide eroded gully, the Devil's Coachroad, which is used to access the top of the crag.

CONDITIONS

South facing so gets plenty of sun.

DIRECTIONS

The crag can be approached from the north or south, which is best depends on the direction you are driving from. The walk in from the south follows the approach for Lower Cove but continues up the Annalong Valley for another kilometre until close to the foot of Slieve Beg.

The approach from the north requires quite a bit of climbing but is slightly shorter. From the Donard carpark in Newcastle follow the track up the Glen River valley to the Slieve Commedagh/Slieve Donard col. Walk down into the valley to the south for 250m until you meet a well eroded track that traverses the slope. Follow this track, known as the Brandy Pad, northwest. Contour across the hillside once you are level with the foot of the crag. See map on page 269.

SOUTH FACE

1 Devil's Rib VD   54m

Wonderful, exposed climbing. Start at the base of the rib marking the left-hand edge of the South Face.
P1 20m Climb onto the rib from the left and up to belay. Climbing directly up the front of the rib is S.
P2 34m The exposed arete, turning the top overhang.
R. Johnston, N. Gault, W. Archer 31/10/1947

The next two routes are accessed by abseil (one 50m required assuming you are leaving it in place) from the stake near the top of The Third Man.

2 **The Third Man** E1 5b   50m

The arete left of Cosmik Debris. Start from the small ledge 3m above and left of the start of Cosmik Debris. Move up via a distinct pocket and out right to a ledge on the arete. Follow the edge over an overlap to a series of ledges. Delicate moves up the blunt arete lead to yet more ledges. Continue up and left over the ledges and follow a pair of cracks to the base of the arete. The superb finish up the arete is well protected.
I. Rea, K. O'Hara April 2006

3 **Cosmik Debris** E1 5b   50m

An amazing route with a big feel. Abseil down to the clean ledge. Climb the corner passing an overlap to a small roof at 15m. Move directly up to the blocky ledge below the crack in the slabby headwall. Follow the crack to the top in a great position.
K. O'Hara, I. Rea 02/11/2006

4 **Burden of Dreams** E3 (5a,5a,6a,4b)   114m

The clean corner on the third pitch is superb.
P1   22m Start at the leftward trending crack are few meters left of the grassy ramp. Climb the crack and flakes to a grassy ramp.
P2   12m Follow another left trending system of flakes to the left edge of the overhang. Traverse right under the overhang until it's possible to cross it at break and then go straight up to the ledge.
P3   40m Climb up to the roof and layback around it on the right. Move up until it's possible to step left into the base of the very steep right-facing corner. Follow this over the roof (sustained) into the niche and continue up to the large ledge.
P4   40m Scramble left up the heather and climb the clean section of rock above.
I. Rea, P. Holmes 23/04/1990

MAIN FACE

5 **Satanic Majesty** E2 (4c,5b)   55m

The second pitch is one of the best in the Mournes. Approach by scrambling up heather on the right.
P1   15m Climb the groove and corner to the large platform.
P2   41m Bridge around the small overhang just above the belay and follow the groove to a small ledge on the right. Move left to the base of the corner. Climb the corner to the overhang and step right to the arete. Move up and left to regain the groove and follow it more easily to the top. Scramble up broken ground to belay.
S. Crymble, M. Curran, D. Chambers 26/03/1973
FFA C. Torrans, S. Billane 1974

6 **Poetic Justice** VS (4b,4b,4b)   80m

A Mournes classic. Sustained interest, exposure and great belays. The first pitch take a crack line up the crest of the large buttress. Start 3m left of the small gully marking the right-hand end of the buttress.

P1 45m Follow the crack and grooves to the bulge. Take a long step left onto a ledge and follow the crack in the nose above. Climb up, step right to the arete and move up on loose blocks to the large grass ledge.

P2 20m Pass grassy blocks and an awkward mantleshelf to an airy ledge on the left. Climb steeply up and right to belay beneath a corner.

P3 15m Follow the corner to the top.

W. Jenkins, C. Moore 08/07/1966

DEVIL'S COACHROAD

The prominent, eroded gully that divides the crag is known as the Devil's Coachroad. The following climbs are found on the north wall of the gully. Watch out for loose rock towards the top.

7 **Parallel Lines** HVS 5a   40m

Ooh, yeah! All right! We're jamming. I wanna jam it with you. We're jamming, jamming, And I hope you like jamming, too.

C. Torrans, C. Sheridan 16/06/1979

8 **Sweetie Mice** HVS 5a   40m

A neglected classic. Climb the corner until forced at a bulge to step right to the arete which is followed more easily to the top.

J. McGuinness, J. Bruce 19/05/1973

MOURNE MAGGIE

On the far right end of the crag is a prominent, clean slab.

9 **Mourne Maggie** HVS 5a   48m

Absorbing climbing with just enough protection. Just possible in one pitch with 50m ropes. Climb up to the ledge at the base of the slab. Climb up and left for 5m before moving right and following the diminishing crack system until a delicate move leads to a shallow scoop. Traverse left below the overhang to the crack at the left-hand end of the overhang which is followed to the top.

K. Quinn, W. Holmes 11/09/1977

THIRD CORNER

8 Agag's Wall VS 4b   30m

Amazing bold climbing. From the left edge of the wall move up and right and continue directly up the middle of the wall. Finish over (4c) or around (4b) the right hand side of the roof or step right (4a). The more direct start is VS 4c.
S. Moorehead, C. Stead 18/06/1967

9 Pillar Variant S (4a,4a)   40m

A very popular classic. See photo on page 236.
P1   25m Climb easily to the ledge at the base of the corner. Move out right and up the steep wall (well protected) to the large ledge.
P2   15m Climb the arete on rounded holds.
S. Moorehead, C. Stead 18/06/1967

FOURTH CORNER

10 **Brewer's Gloom** S (3c,4a,3c)   45m

A fantastic route that weaves its way up the wall.
P1   18m Climb the wall and move right around the edge. Climb the corner and
move right to belay.
P2   12m Mantleshelf right and traverse right around an airy corner to belay on the
ledge.
P3   15m Climb the steep wall on good holds, moving left at top.
P. Grindley and party 18/11/1961

11 **Swing Low** E2 (5b,3c)   43m

Superb, steep, strenuous and safe.
P1   28m Bridge up the recess and move slightly left to a ledge. Follow the steep
crack to the chimney and thrash up it to a belay on the ledge.
P2   15m As for P3 of Brewer's Gloom.
M. Smith, R. Cole 09/09/1978

First Corner

Second Corner

Third Corner

Fourth Corner

East Face

County Down

LOWER COVE
APPROACH **60 minutes**
ROCK **Granite**
D-S **2** - HS-HVS **4** - E1-E3 **6** - E4+ **2**

The relatively flat walk-in, large selection of routes at all grades and excellent, well protected climbing make Lower Cover one of the best and most popular crags in the Mournes.

CONDITIONS

South facing and reasonably sheltered from the wind.

DIRECTIONS

From the Carrick Little carpark follow the track north passing Annalong Wood. Just beyond the river crossing is a fork in the track. Take the right branch and follow it up the valley to Lower Cove.

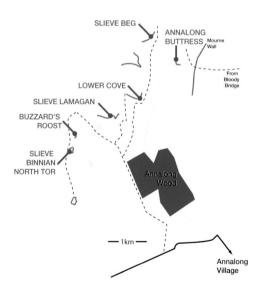

SLIEVE BEG

ANNALONG BUTTRESS

Mourne Wall

From Bloody Bridge

LOWER COVE

SLIEVE LAMAGAN

BUZZARD'S ROOST

SLIEVE BINNIAN NORTH TOR

Annalong Wood

1km

Annalong Village

FACING PAGE Damian O'Sullivan on Overdue E2 5c (see page 270). Photo by Dave Ayton.

FIRST CORNER

1 **First Corner** HS 4b   25m

Climb the arete to a ledge on the left where you step left and move up for 3m before returning to the arete and finishing up it. Staying on the arete is slightly harder (4c).
F. Devlin, J. McGrath 30/06/1965

2 **Meat Grinder** E2 5c   25m

Safe but exposed. Climb the steep wall to the first crack. Move right to the crack above (crux) and finish more easily.
P. Douglas, M. Smith, W. Holmes July 1980

3 **Overdue** E2 5c   25m

Well protected with a long reach at the crux. Climb the shallow groove, pass the overlaps and move left finishing up the arete. See photo on page 268.
A. McQuoid, M. Henry May 1979
FFA T. Irvine, J MacGarry June 1979

4 **Dot's Delight** HVS 4c   40m

A bold, exposed route with lots of traversing so make sure to protect the second and watch out for rope drag. Move diagonally right then up to a peg (optional belay) at the overlap. Traverse left to a large ledge and finish easily but airily up the wall.
P. Kavannagh, F. Devlin 29/11/1964

SECOND CORNER

5 **Gynocrat** HVS 5a   30m

A great line with adequate protection. Climb through the overlaps to the crack which
is followed to a ledge. A hard move off the ledge leads to easier ground. At the top
either finish right or more directly up the wall.
D. Stelfox, A. McQuoid February 1980

6 **Aristocrat** E1 5b   35m

An intimidating line up the edge of the buttress. Make a delicate traverse right to the
groove which is followed to the heather ledge. Climb the steep wall directly above.
One hard move leads to easier ground.
A. McQuoid, A. Currans 27/04/1980

7 **Graffiti Limbo** E4 (5b,6b)   47m

Highly technical moves and steep, perfect rock.
P1   12m Climb the groove and make a tricky move up and right to the large belay
ledge in the cave.
P2   35m From the right edge of the cave move up and right to a good rest below
a white hanging slab topped by a roof. Gain the slab with difficulty on its left side.
Climb the bulge above (strenuous) to the horizontal breaks which are followed right
to a large grass ledge. Finish up the blunt arete.
E. Cooper, A. Moles September 1990

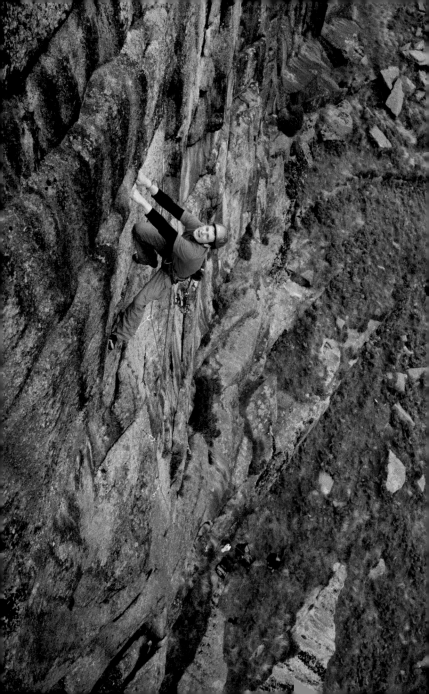

THE EAST FACE

The very impressive, steep East Face lies just around the corner from the Fourth Corner.

12 Les Jeunes Filles en Jupes d'Ete E2 5b   30m

Steep and sustained. Also known as 'The French Route'. Move directly up the steep wall to a ledge and peg at 15m. From here move up and left to the ledge below the roof. Finish by this, starting from the left-hand side of the ledge.
A. Currans, A. McQuoid 04/05/1980

13 A Winter's Tale E3 6a   30m

Worth checking out the condition of the pegs before an ascent. Start 5m right of Les Jeunes Filles and follow a line of pegs to a ledge (crux). Use the flake crack above to reach another ledge. Move up and slightly left until forced back right to good holds and the top.
E. Cooper 01/11/1988

14 The 5th Ape E5 6a   30m

A tricky start and a steep pumpy finish. Start under a ledge and plinth. Gain the plinth with care and move into the thin, right-facing layback flake on the left. Follow this to a good rest. A tricky move gains the huge flake up and right. Mantel onto the jug above using flat undercuts (crux). Stretch up to the break and trend left into and up the hanging groove to finish. See photo on facing page.
D. O'Neill 12/10/2008

FACING PAGE Pete Whittaker on The 5th Ape E5 6a. Photo by Mike Hutton.

County Down
ANNALONG BUTTRESS
APPROACH **75 minutes**
ROCK **Granite**
D-S **7** - HS-HVS **6** - E1-E3 **0** - E4+ **0**

A small but attractive buttress sitting high on the eastern side of the Annalong Valley. Offers a good variety of generally well protected routes on good, clean rock.

CONDITIONS

Clean and quick to dry.

DIRECTIONS

Park at the carpark 6km south of Newcastle on the A2. Slog up the Bloody Bridge Track to the Mourne Wall. Cross the wall and follow the path for 250m before heading west for 350m to the top of the crag. See map on page 269.

1 **Sherpa Conifer** S 3c
25m

Tricky enough and surprisingly quite airy. Follow the left-hand recess then step right into the quartz pot using a high hidden jug on the right. Finish up and left.
P. Gribbon, J. Madill May 1952

2 **Cum Marte** VS 4c
25m

An intimidating line but not as bad as it looks but still not a pushover.
R. A. Court, A. Matthews, R. Cox 12/06/1965

3 **Hanging Corner** S 3c
21m

A fine route but prone to dampness however this only adds to the fun.
M. McMurray, B. Blakie June 1949

4 **Bilberry Bhutia** VD
21m

Climb the wall to a ledge at two-thirds height. Move right to the deep crack at the grass ledge and climb past the left-hand side of the nose.
Unknown

5 **Thin Crack** VS 4c
25m

The classic of the crag. Positive, well protected climbing up the prominent crack.
C. Moore, G. Earnshaw June 1964

6 **Warsaw Convention** VS 4c
27m

Another quality crack climb. Follow the flakes up and right to the crack which is climbed to the top.
P. Gribbon and party 1962

7 **P is for Paddy** VS 4b   30m

Not quite in the same league as the previous two routes. Climb the wall on small holds, and continue up the crack to finish as for Warsaw Convention (4c) or step down and right to the ledge.
J. McKenzie, P. Gargan

8 **Minerva** HS 4b   32m

Climb the wall to the crack which becomes easier after the grass ledge near the top.
Unknown

9 **Lacuna** HVS 4c   35m

Low in the grade but bold near the start then easier and pleasant after this. Climb easily to the quartz flake at 3m and continue to the horizontal crack. Move left, then up the cracks to the grassy ledge, 12m of easy climbing leads to the top.
C. Torrans, C. Torrans June 1980

10 **Spanish Flea** S (3c,3c)   45m

A very good varied outing with steady difficulties.
P1 22m Climb the crack to the triangular block. Swing right around this to a recess. Move back left to the cracks and follow them to the grassy ledge.
P2 23m Climb the short left-facing corner and step right to the top of the block. Thoughtful moves up the slab above lead to the top. Belay at the block 10m back.
W. Jenkins, W. Martin, B. Hedley 09/10/1966

11 **Springtime** S (4a,3b)   45m

A short but delightful exercise in jamming.
P1 12m Jam up the good crack and belay at recess.
P2 33m Bridge up the recess above and step right into cracks, follow them to the top. Belay at the block 10m back.
I. Brown, C. Moore March 1964

12 **South Route** D   48m

Start at the crack 2m left of the right-hand edge.
P1 15m Climb the crack and follow the lower ramp to the recess.
P2 33m As for P2 of Springtime.
D. McMurray, B. Blakie June 1964

13 **Britton's Route** D   45m

Start as for South Route.
P1 15m Climb the crack to the upper ramp which is followed leftward to a corner.
P2 30m Up the corner and follow cracks on the right to the top, moving left or right around a short wall to finish. Belay about 10m back from the edge.
D. Britton, C. Moore June 1964

ROUTE INDEX

REFERENCES

Guidebooks

Climbs in the Burren and Aran Islands by Peter Owens, published by Mountaineering Ireland.
Dalkey Quarry, edited by Ronan Browner and Howard Hebblethwaithe, published by Mountaineering Ireland.
Fair Head Rock Climbing Guide edited by Calvin Torrans and Clare Sheridan, published by Mountaineering Ireland.
Fair Head Rock Climbing Guide by Ricky Bell and Craig Hiller, published by Mountaineering Ireland.
From High Places by Adrian Hendroff, published by The History Press.
Macgillycuddy's Reeks by John Murray, published by The Dermot Bouchier-Hayes Commemoration Trust.
Munster's Mountains by Denis Lynch, published by Collins Press.
Rock Climbs in Donegal edited by Alan Tees, published by Mountaineering Ireland.
Rock Climbing in Ireland edited by Calvin Torrans and Dawson Stelfox, published by Constable.
Rock Climbs in the Mourne Mountains by Simon Moore, Craig Hiller and Ricky Bell, published by Mountaineering Ireland.
The Ridges of England, Wales and Ireland by Dan Bailey, published by Circerone
Wicklow Rock Climbing Guide edited by Joe Lyons, published by Mountaineering Ireland.

Websites

For updates, corrections, and a digital map of every climbing area listed in this book check out www.rockClimbingInIreland.com

Irish Climbing Online, Route Database
wiki.climbing.ie/index.php/Irish_Climbing_Route_Database

List of climbing walls in Ireland
www.mountaineering.ie/Climbing/ClimbingWalls

Mournes Climbers
www.mournesclimbers.com

Colmcille Climbers Club hosts a very comprehensive database of Donegal routes
www.colmcilleclimbers.com

Iain Miller's website has detailed PDF guides for every area in Donegal
www.colmcilleclimbers.com

FACING PAGE Dave Ayton on Indecent Assault E8 6c, Dalkey Quarry, Dublin. Photo by Conor Doherty.

ADVERTISERS

Three Rock Books would like to thank all the following advertisers who helped support this guidebook.

THIS SPREAD Dave MacLeod on Divided Years E9 6c, Buzzard's Roost, Mournes (see page 253). Photo by Dave Brown - Hot Aches Productions.

ACKNOWLEDGMENTS

All guidebooks rely to some extent on the information that is already out there and I'm indebted to all the guidebook authors who have volunteered their time over the years to produce the Mountaineering Ireland definitive guidebooks.

I received a huge amount of feedback in the process of writing this guide from far too many people to mention each individually. Thanks to everyone who offered their thoughts on route selection, grades, descriptions, and especially to those who read draft chapters.

Thanks to all the photographers who contributed photos - Juraj Navratil, Ben Ditto, Thomas Prebble, Seán Martin, Stephen McGowan, Barry Denton, Damon Corso, Peter McMahon, Pat Nolan, Dave Ayton, Daniel Moore, Marek Przybylski, Stephen Carson, Iain Miller, Iain Webster, Gareth McCormack, Michael O'Dwyer, Jeremy Colandairaj, Pedro Pimentel, René Caroline Temple, James Dunn, Mike Hutton, Michelle O'Loughlin, Dave Brown, Conor Doherty. Special thanks to Richard Creagh who granted me full access to his archive of great photos and Craig Hiller for his amazing cover shot.

I'm very grateful to everyone at Mountaineering Ireland for their help and encouragement with this project.

Thanks to the companies that advertised - Alpine Sports, Awesome Walls, Gravity Climbing Centre, Great Outdoors. Please give them your custom.

Finally I would like to thank my family - Jenny, Hazel and Milo - for their support throughout this project.